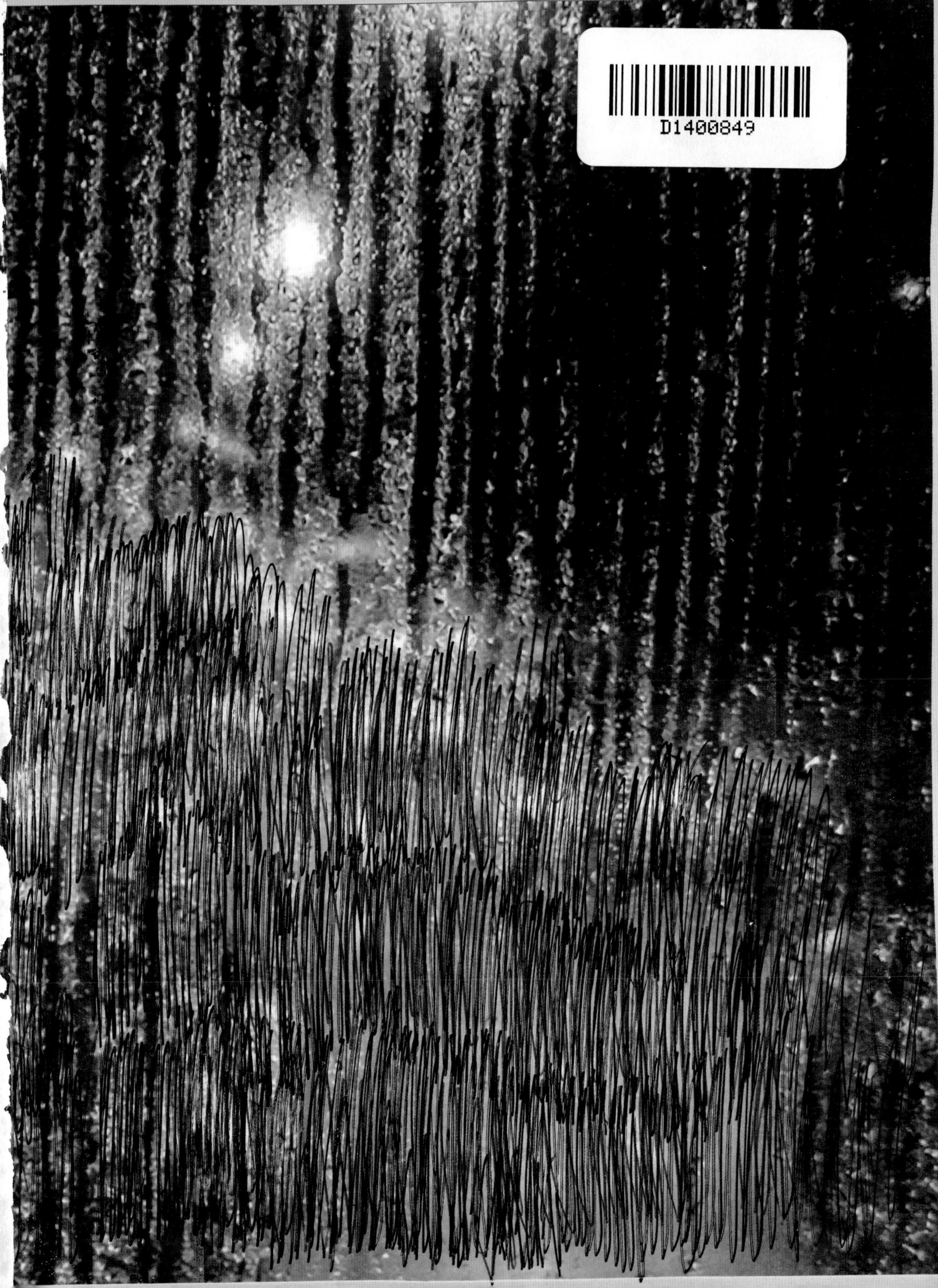

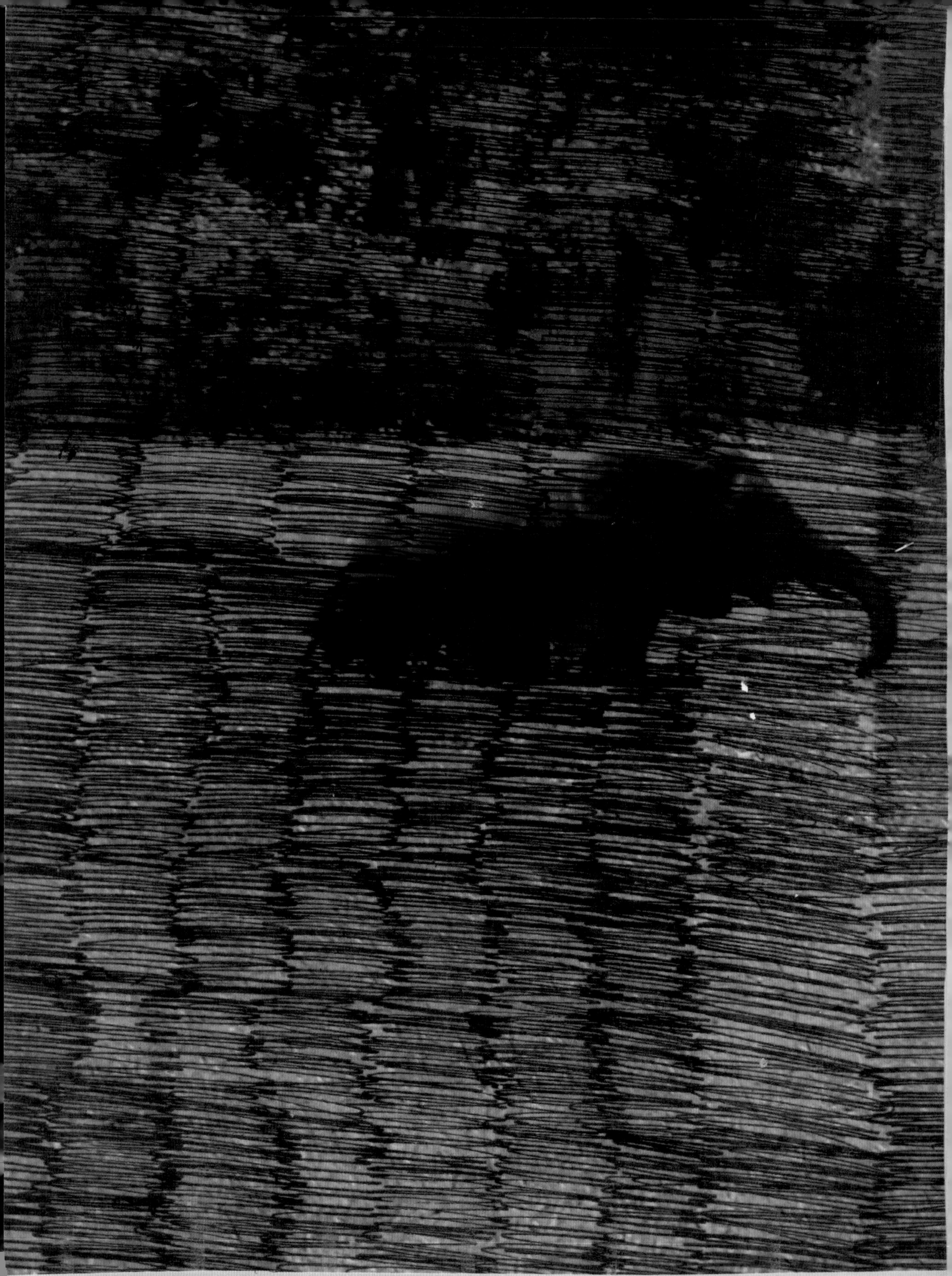

I'm here. In the chaotic immigration line, it's clear that there are no tourists, just NGO workers. They are elegant in white and khaki, but wild-eyed. My guide is waiting with her jeep. The car is all rust and duct tape. We drive into the anarchy of Lilongwe, the capital city, and straight to the downtown bank machine. Everyone seems to drive jeeps - a gray haze of pollution curtains the bright sun. As we step out of the car, I hear the voices - "OI! MUZUNGU!" Hey! White girl! Men and boys surround us. It's too easy an observation to note that they're barefoot, with torn pants sliding off jutting hips. They close in as I punch the buttons on the broken machine. There's this kid who looks about nine, coated in dirt. He is basically naked, with ragged beige shorts that only really cover his thighs. His eyes are glassy, as if he's been sniffing glue.

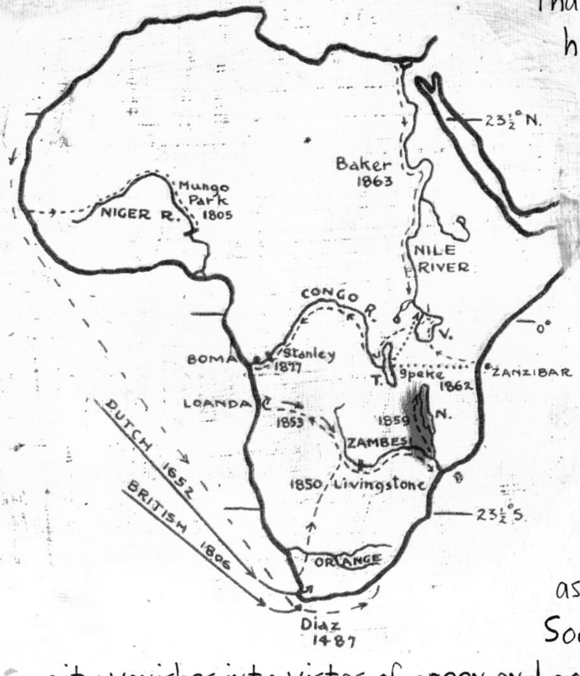
Mungo
Park
1805
NIGER R.
Baker
1863
23½° N.
NILE
RIVER
CONGO R.
V.
0°
BOMA
Stanley
1877
T.
Speke
1862
ZANZIBAR
LOANDA
1853
1859
N.
ZAMBES
1850
Livingstone
23½° S.
DUTCH 1652
BRITISH 1806
ORANGE
Diaz
1487

We climb into the jeep and roar away, covering the men with road dust. "It's just the way it is here," says the guide, seeing me look back at the boy as we drive away.

Soon the melee of the city vanishes into vistas of green and gold maize fields.

I'm staying on a working dairy farm that is also a country lodge. Rolling hills slope and turn back on themselves like sand dunes. Sitting on the veranda off of the dining room, I watch the sunrise. Hotel workers move like shadows around the white guests, lighting citronella candles.

We're going to travel with a group of American activists today, to see some rural villages and meet the Malawian heads of aid projects designed to help communities care for themselves. Since most people here speak only Chichewa, a translator has been arranged, but - she is not able to work today.

Thankfully, there is a replacement.

She's a tall woman from Zimbabwe with cropped hair and tight, faded jeans. Her English is perfect and she has this so-what fuck-you look on her face. She doesn't seem to have any inhibitions - she sleeps with women sometimes, men sometimes, so what? Who cares that homosexuality is illegal in this country?

She notices that I'm looking at her belly, which hangs over her waistband like soup boiling over a pot. "My stomach is big," she says, "because of the ARVs" - the antiretroviral drugs used to treat HIV. "I also have bad skin. This is another side effect." She snaps her tongue in the middle of her mouth. She is always hungry - another side effect of the ARVs. She loves - LOVES! - white bread. In fact, she loves a lot of things at the grocery store, as she piles soap, soft drinks, and condiments on the conveyer belt, hands on hips, eyebrows raised, waiting for me to pay. Back in the jeep, she devours a loaf of bread, spraying white crumbs onto my lap.

By the time we get to the village, the car has steamed up and smells like yeast. We are taken to a hut where local NGOs tell us what they are doing for their villages. The villages are vanishing: HIV/AIDS, tuberculosis, malaria. There are charts, pieces of yellowed paper with lots of figures on them. The handwriting is in old-fashioned male scrawl. Did we know:

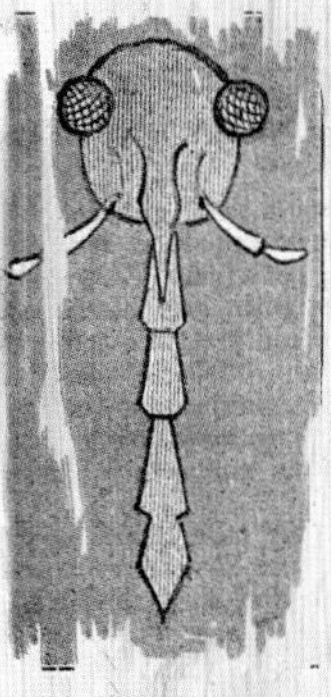

- There are 1.6 medical doctors for every 100,000 people
- Almost 60% of people living with HIV are women
- Average life expectancy in Malawi is 46 years
- There are 550,000 AIDS orphans in the country
- We need $$$ to continue running our program
- Would we also consider taking a box of local gemstones to sell from our homes to raise funds?

We are escorted to our cars. The afternoon sun is making the plastic seats burn my ass. I wish I had sandals on and my stomach is making loud noises from hunger. We pull into another village and are shown to a set of folding chairs. The whole village is assembled in front of us, staring. Some people smile - I've never seen such wide, beautiful smiles. Huge eyes that light up with joy so fresh it looks like it could smudge.

"Welcome, people from America . . ." says the village chief, a large man with many wives. For the next 45 minutes, he and others list the reasons that their village needs money. They know that they don't have a lot of time - we will be gone in a matter of minutes and this is their chance to show us that they desperately need money. Their urgency is heartbreaking. But I can't connect with any of these statistics. A statistic is forgettable. It's never going to move you the way human contact can.

It's hot here. So hot. Rivulets of sweat travel down my chest. I have been looking at the clouds a lot since arriving in Malawi. I've never seen clouds like these before. They are stark white and form the most awesome shapes. Their lining is truly a silver color against the backdrop of blue, and it is easy to get lost in them and create magical worlds. One of the clouds looks like a Komodo dragon. ". . . and thank you, American donors. For coming to our village."

At last we have a few minutes to tour the village, a cluster of mud huts with thatch roofs. Most have no furniture inside. Just a maize bag to sleep on. I lag behind the group, hoping I'll have a chance to speak with a 16-year-old girl who was introduced as an example of a "child-headed family." At age 12 she lost both her parents and became head of the family for her nine brothers and sisters.

"Can I speak with you? Maybe we can sit over there by the field and hang out?"

I look at my translator to say this in Chichewa.

"Hi . . . can I speak with you? Maybe . . . we can sit over there . . . and hang out?" My translator is repeating my words. Very slowly. In English.

She doesn't speak Chichewa.

We go from village to village, and I feel like I'm watching a UNICEF documentary from my car window.

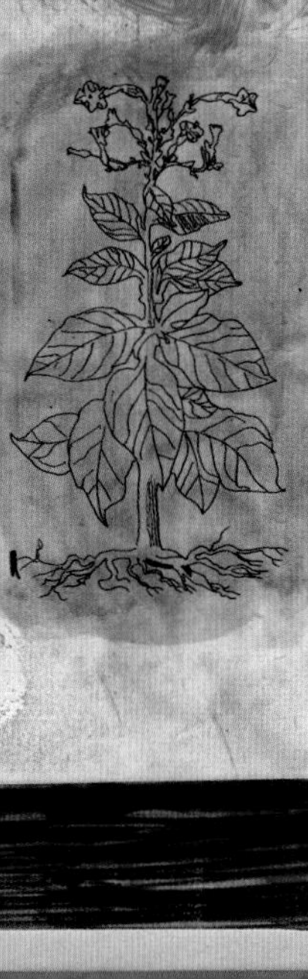

The owner of the country lodge is named Liam. He's like a building about to collapse under its own weight. He must be over 6 feet tall and has thick legs with veins that look like they're about to burst. His feet are always swollen and he limps. "It's the gout," he says. His thick South African accent sounds like it is mixed with gravel and bees. He shrugs off everything. Malaria - "like the common cold, mate." Bilharzia - "I'll be fine." He quit drinking a while ago but still smokes Stuyvesant cigarettes.

One day years ago, he moved his tall feline wife and their daughter from South Africa to Malawi. He wanted to be in a quieter place. He built the lodge from the ground up and created an organic farm and a large cow pasture. It's well run and safe. Standing in the gardens, you could easily believe you were in Byron Bay, the lush hippie mecca in Australia. Step inside the guarded gates and all of the day's dirt and sadness can be scrubbed off with a hot shower just in time for an evening cocktail with other Caucasian guests.

It's night, sticky and hot. Sometimes, a breeze comes in a rush and I open my mouth so I can cool my insides. Malarial mosquitoes buzz near my ears and the crease of my knees. In the blackness, the whites of people's eyes and the iridescent wings of insects are all you can really see.

Liam is telling a story: A friend of his is driving home one night. No streetlights, terrible country roads, impossible to make out anything around you. Maybe his friend has had

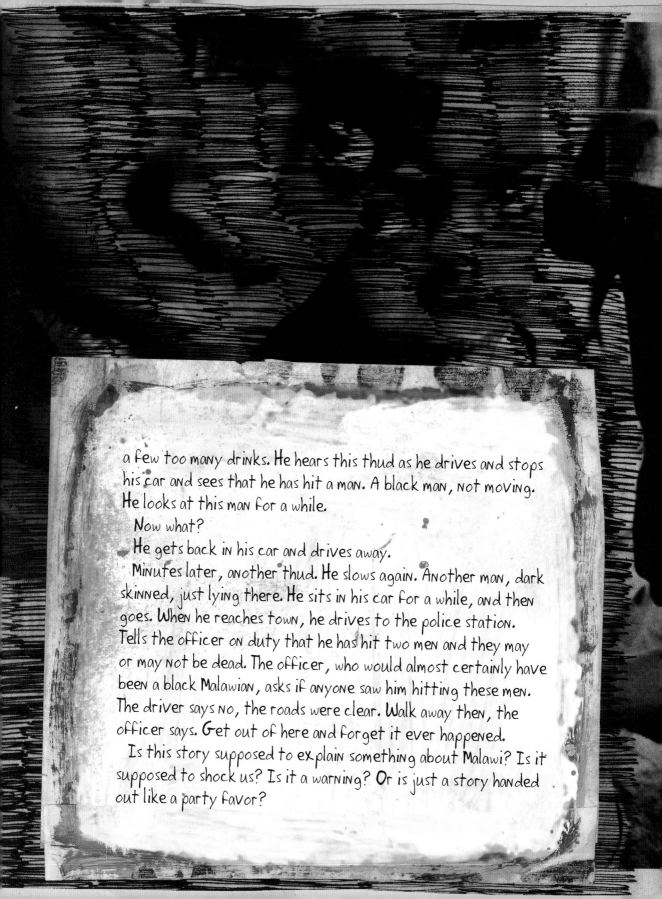

a few too many drinks. He hears this thud as he drives and stops
his car and sees that he has hit a man. A black man, not moving.
He looks at this man for a while.

Now what?

He gets back in his car and drives away.

Minutes later, another thud. He slows again. Another man, dark
skinned, just lying there. He sits in his car for a while, and then
goes. When he reaches town, he drives to the police station.
Tells the officer on duty that he has hit two men and they may
or may not be dead. The officer, who would almost certainly have
been a black Malawian, asks if anyone saw him hitting these men.
The driver says no, the roads were clear. Walk away then, the
officer says. Get out of here and forget it ever happened.

Is this story supposed to explain something about Malawi? Is it
supposed to shock us? Is it a warning? Or is just a story handed
out like a party favor?

CHATTERBOX

BOOK

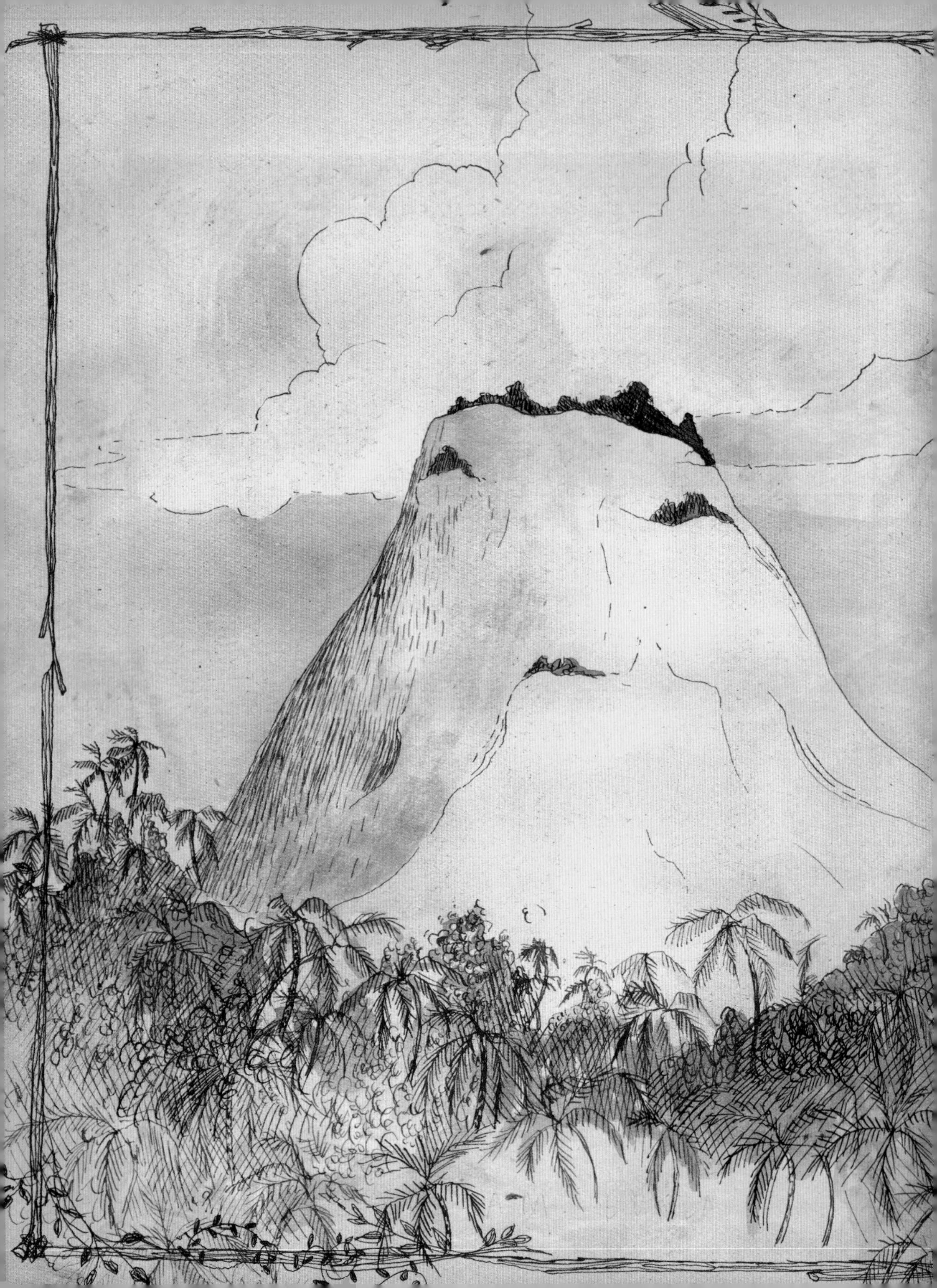

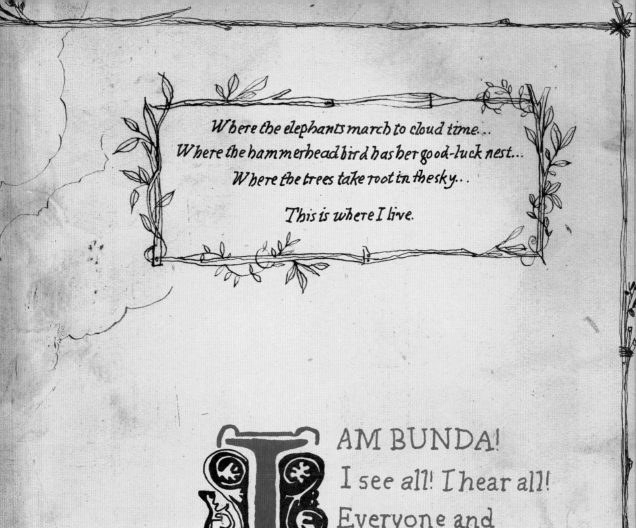

Where the elephants march to cloud time...
Where the hammerhead bird has her good-luck nest...
Where the trees take root in the sky...

This is where I live.

I AM BUNDA!
I see all! I hear all!
Everyone and
everything for a
thousand miles!
I see even the lizard that lives in
the president's bedroom!
I hear even the beating heart of
the baby that will be born!
I see it all! I hear it all!

Do you know it all, Mr. Bunda?

Ha! I would laugh but it would shake the people from their huts in a thousand villages.

No, I don't know it all. I am not a know-it-all. I am a mountain. I am only a small mountain.

I don't know when the baby will be born. I don't know where the baby will be born. I don't know what name they will give her.

But I hear her.

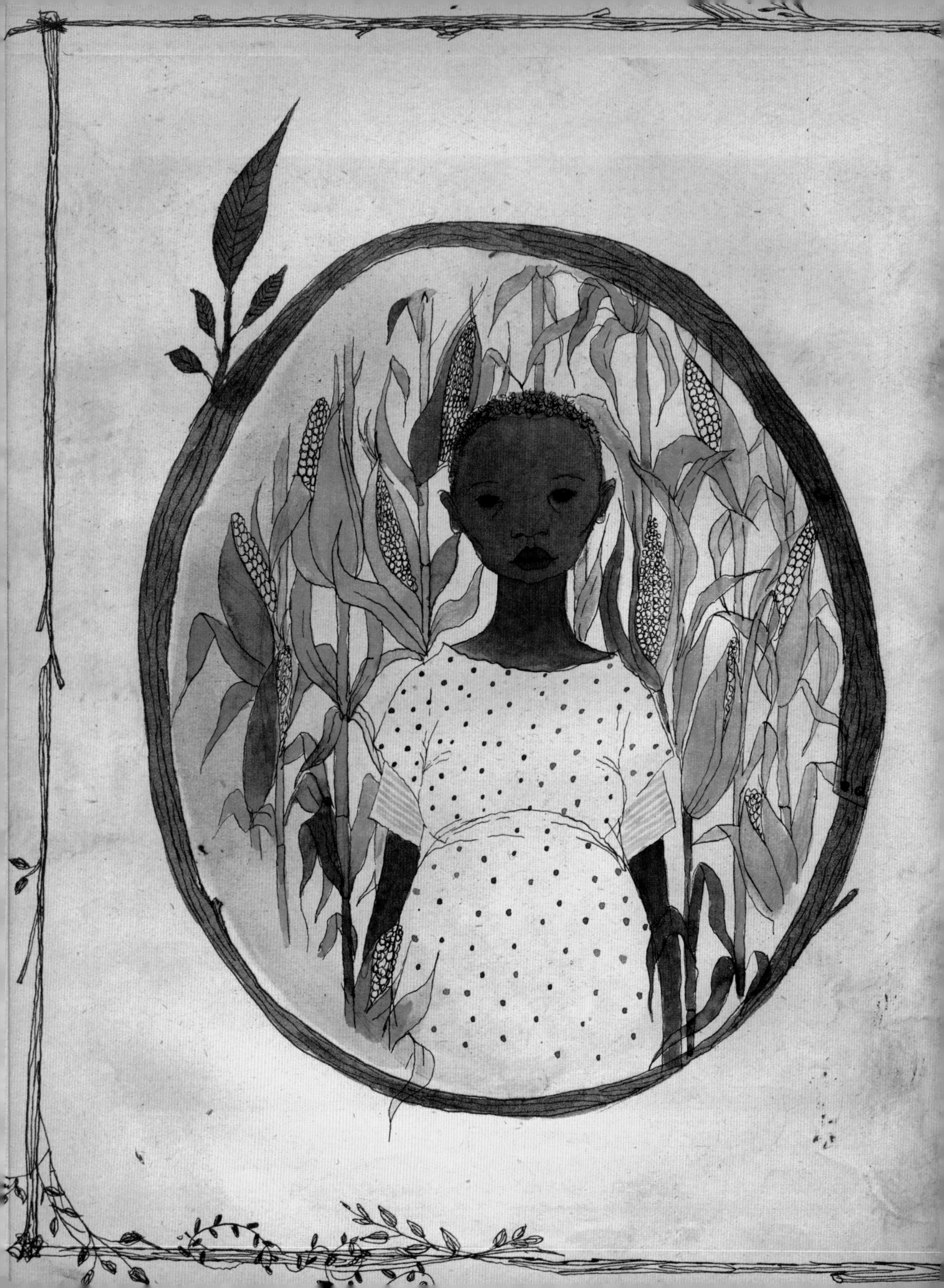

I see Mama!

She carries life inside her. She carries death inside her too. Mama carries the wasting disease.

Will the baby be born with the wasting disease? I do not know. No one can know! Not even the highest mountain can know. Not even Mount Mulanje!

Mama worries about her baby. She is worrying all the time. But today she is only waiting. Maybe today the baby will be born!

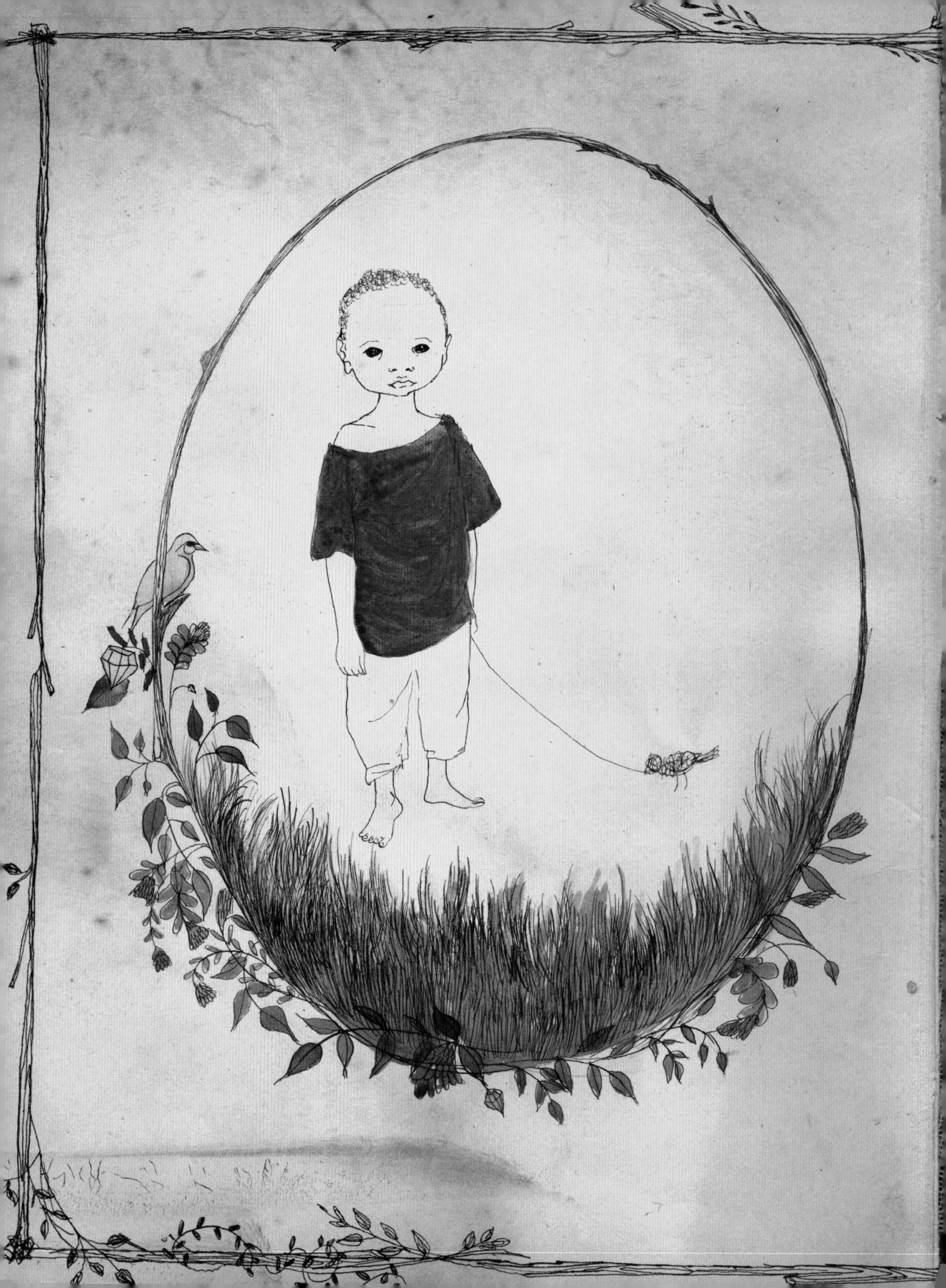

Who will come to see the new baby?

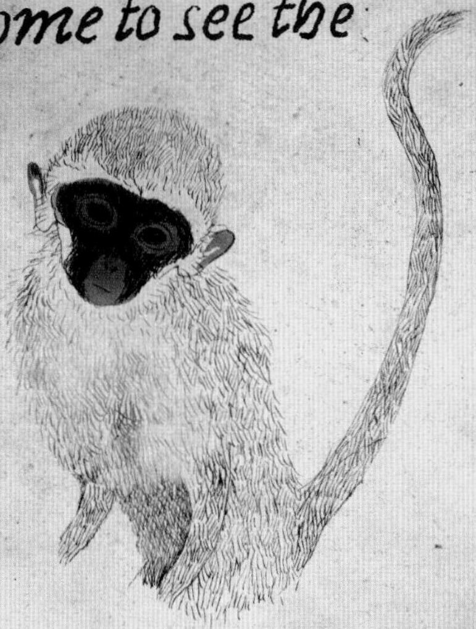

So many people will come!

The little boy Lazarus will come to see the baby.

Lazarus has three teeth. He is learning to smile.

He lives in the village where Mama was born. He lives sometimes here, sometimes there. His father is dead. His mother is dead.

The wasting disease?

Yes, the wasting disease.

Lazarus is always hungry. But Lazarus will come!

And Love will come to see the baby. Do you
know Love? You can see it in his face. Love can't
hear. Love can't talk. What a trouble it is to be
Love! All day long he chases the minibuses in the
village! The people on the bus laugh and laugh.
Love will come to see the new baby.

Love has a sister. Her name is Gift. She loves to spin! Sometimes she spins around the world. Sometimes the world spins around her. She feels like she is being carried away in the beak of a marabou stork!

The people on the street laugh and laugh.

Gift will come to see the baby too.

Oh! I hear the baby moving!
I would smile, but it would split the world
like a peeled banana.

A peeled banana! Mmm!

There go Doubt and Blessing,
the sisters.

They remember when Mama was a teacher in the
village.

Doubt tries to write a poem for the new baby.
~ What a headache I have! ~ she says.
Doubt has ten little brothers and sisters to feed! Her father is dead. Her mother was sent to a village far away.

The wasting disease?

Yes, the wasting disease.

Blessing is fed up with her sister Doubt. ~ She is worrying all the time! She is just so serious. Look at her! ~ says Blessing.

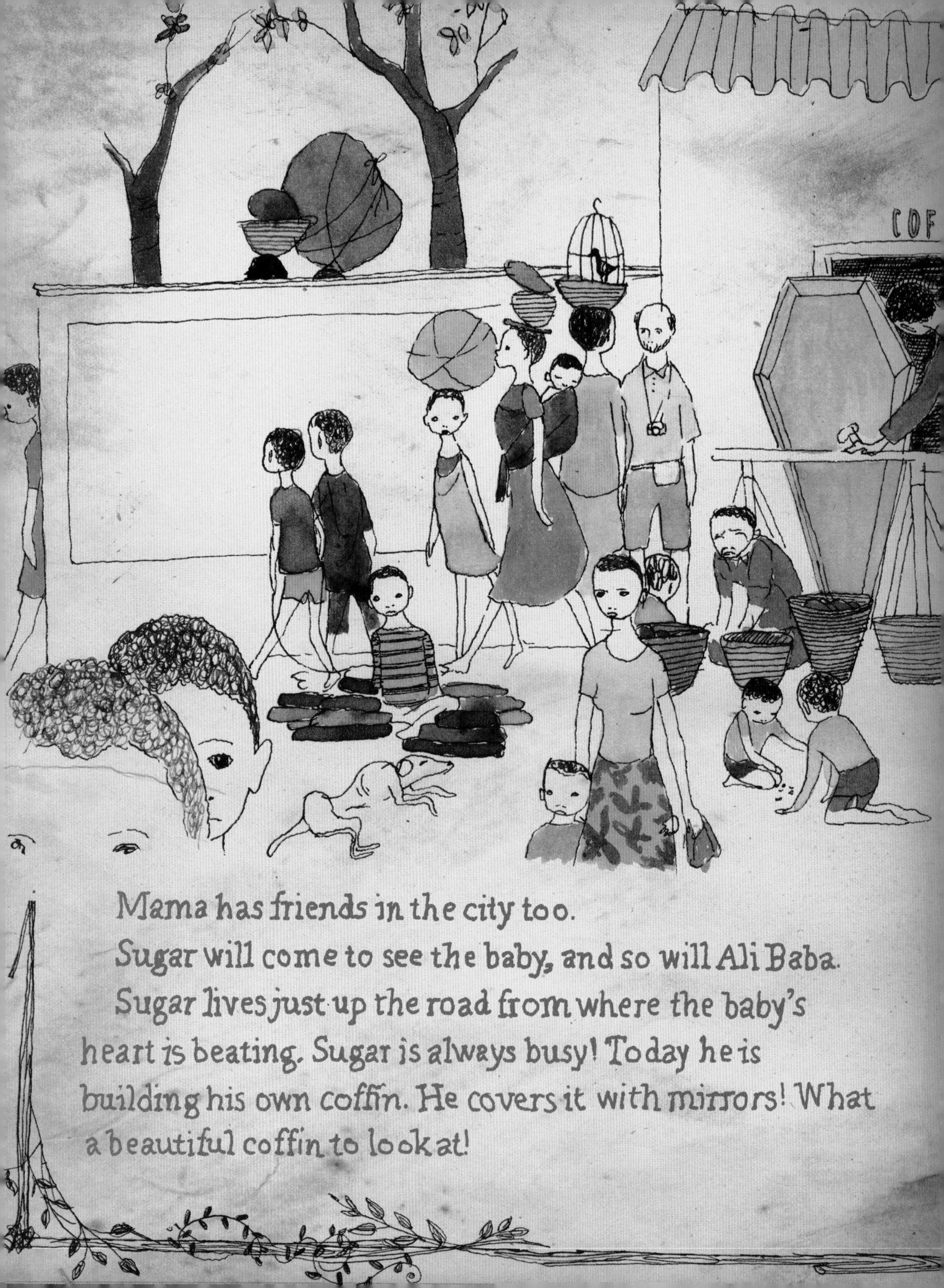
COF

Mama has friends in the city too.

Sugar will come to see the baby, and so will Ali Baba.

Sugar lives just up the road from where the baby's heart is beating. Sugar is always busy! Today he is building his own coffin. He covers it with mirrors! What a beautiful coffin to look at!

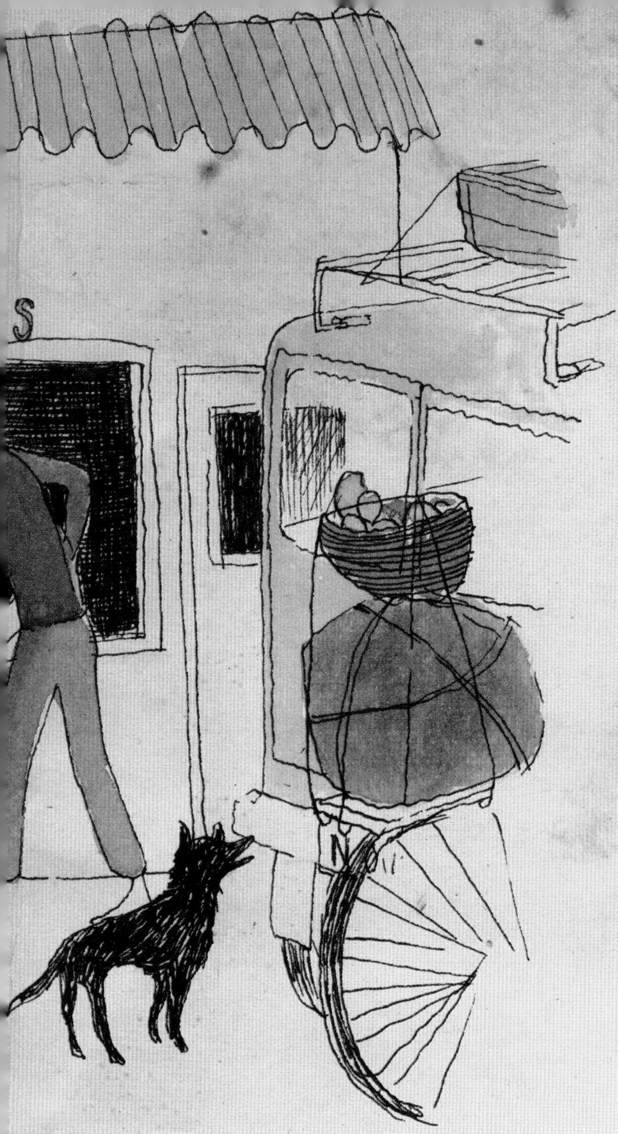

Ali Baba lives in the city too. He sells cloth in the market. He used to live with his uncle. Then one day his uncle beat him with a greasy knotty rope.

Now Ali Baba sleeps beneath the bench in the market where the telephone lady sits.

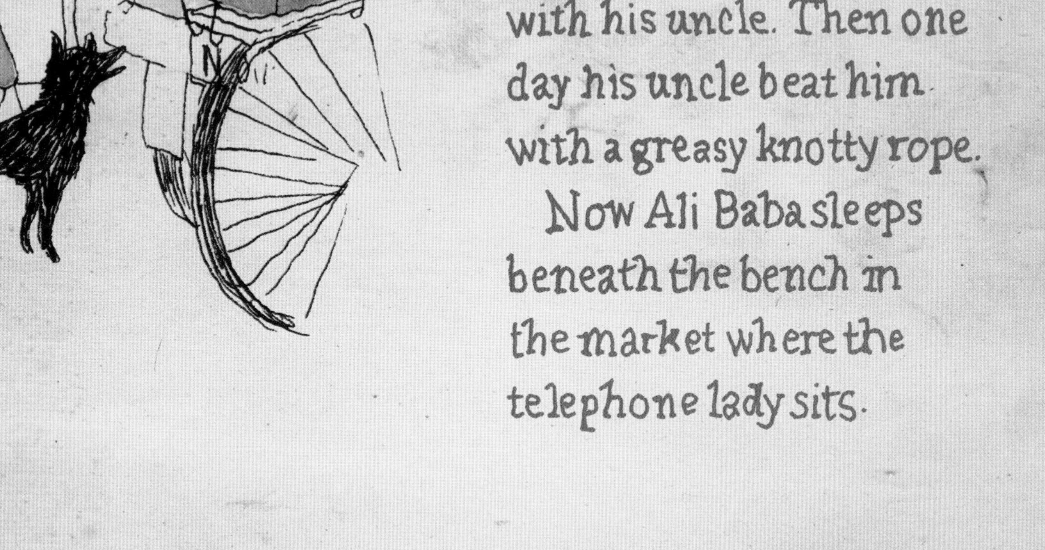

Even Krystal knows Mama!
They played together when
they were two little girls.

Now Mama cleans
in Krystal's house. And
Mama cooks in Krystal's
kitchen. And Mama works
in Krystal's garden.
    Maybe Krystal will ride
her horse to see the new
baby!

Wait. Can you hear?

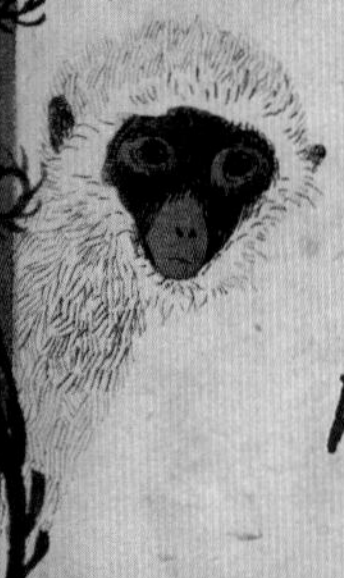

I am only a vervet monkey! What I hear is a ripe mango falling in the forest!

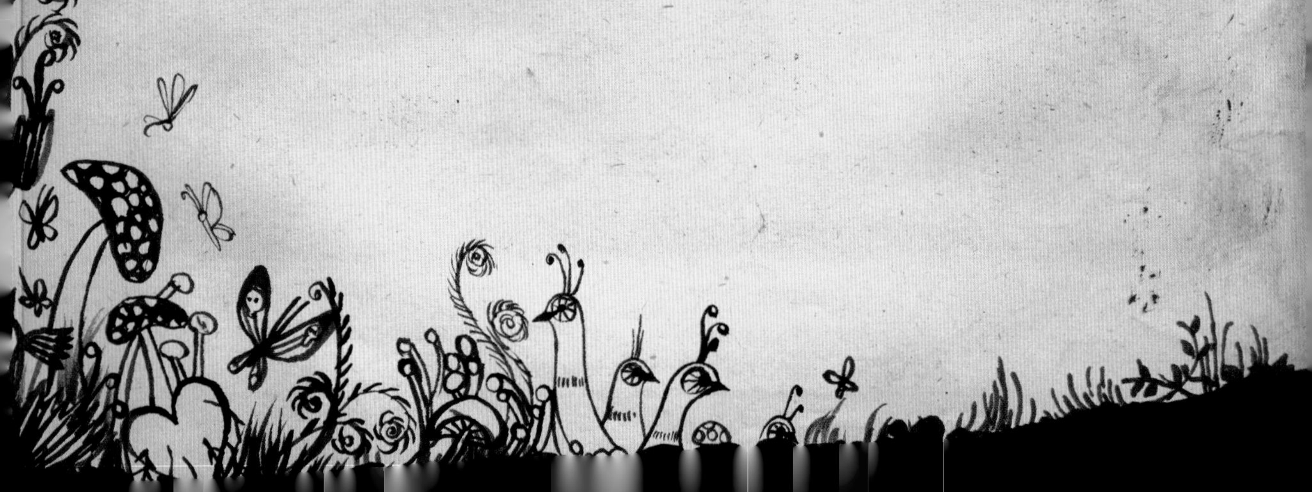

The baby is coming! It sounds like the milky way spilling out of the sky!

Mama is ready to go to the hospital. Oscar will pedal the bicycle ambulance.

And away go Mama and Oscar. It's bumpy!

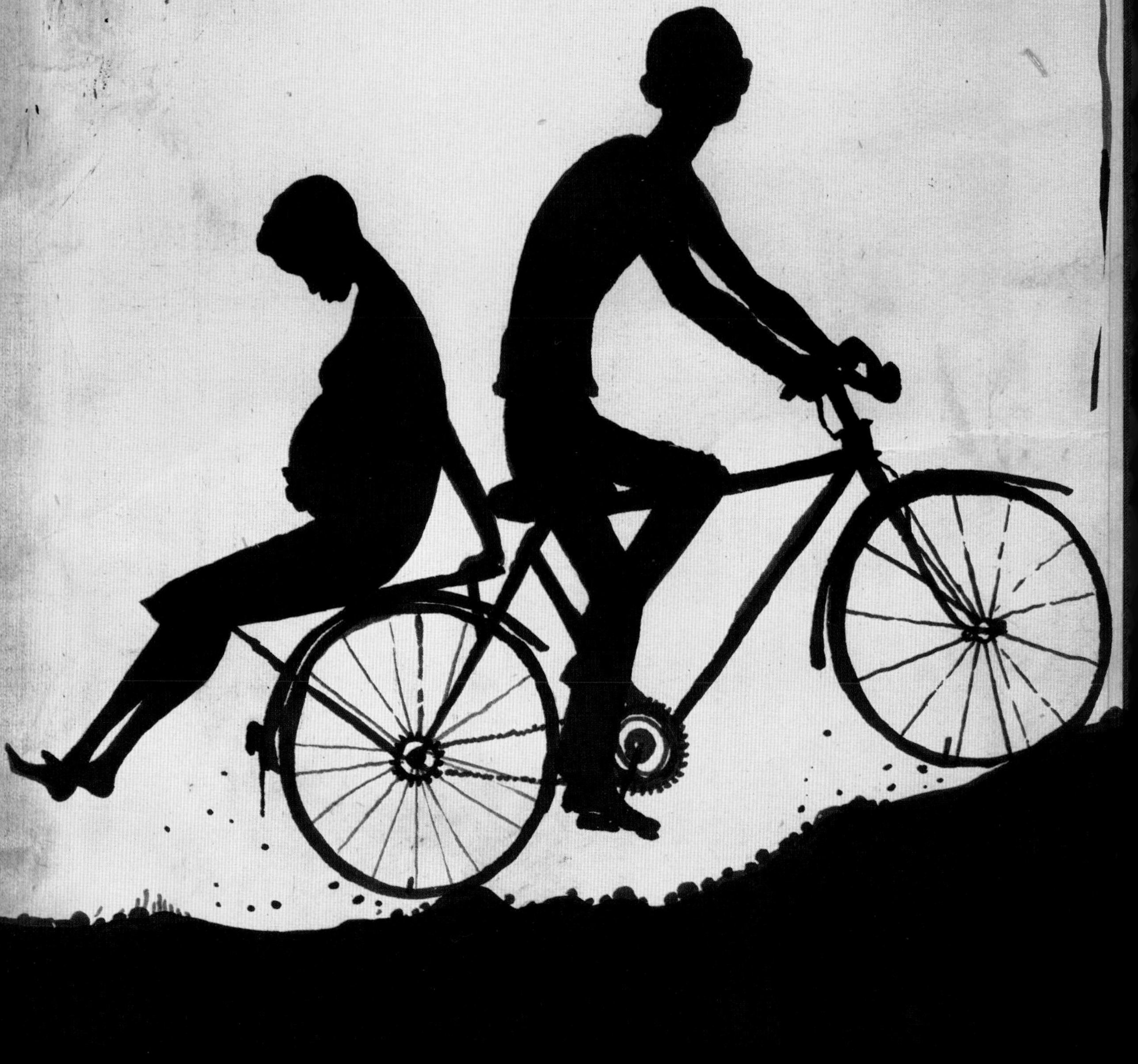

Everyone knows that the baby will come soon.
Everyone is coming to see the new baby!

Lazarus walks the trail beside the river.
He imagines he is eating a big bowl of nsima.
He imagines he is eating a plate full of ngumbi.
He imagines he is a crocodile with his three new teeth!

Love tries to get onto the minibus, but no one will let him!

Oh, he is angry! He chases the bus through the market and slaps on the sides!

The people on the bus laugh and laugh.

Gift is walking to the city when she hears magical music coming over the fields. She follows it like she would follow a butterfly.

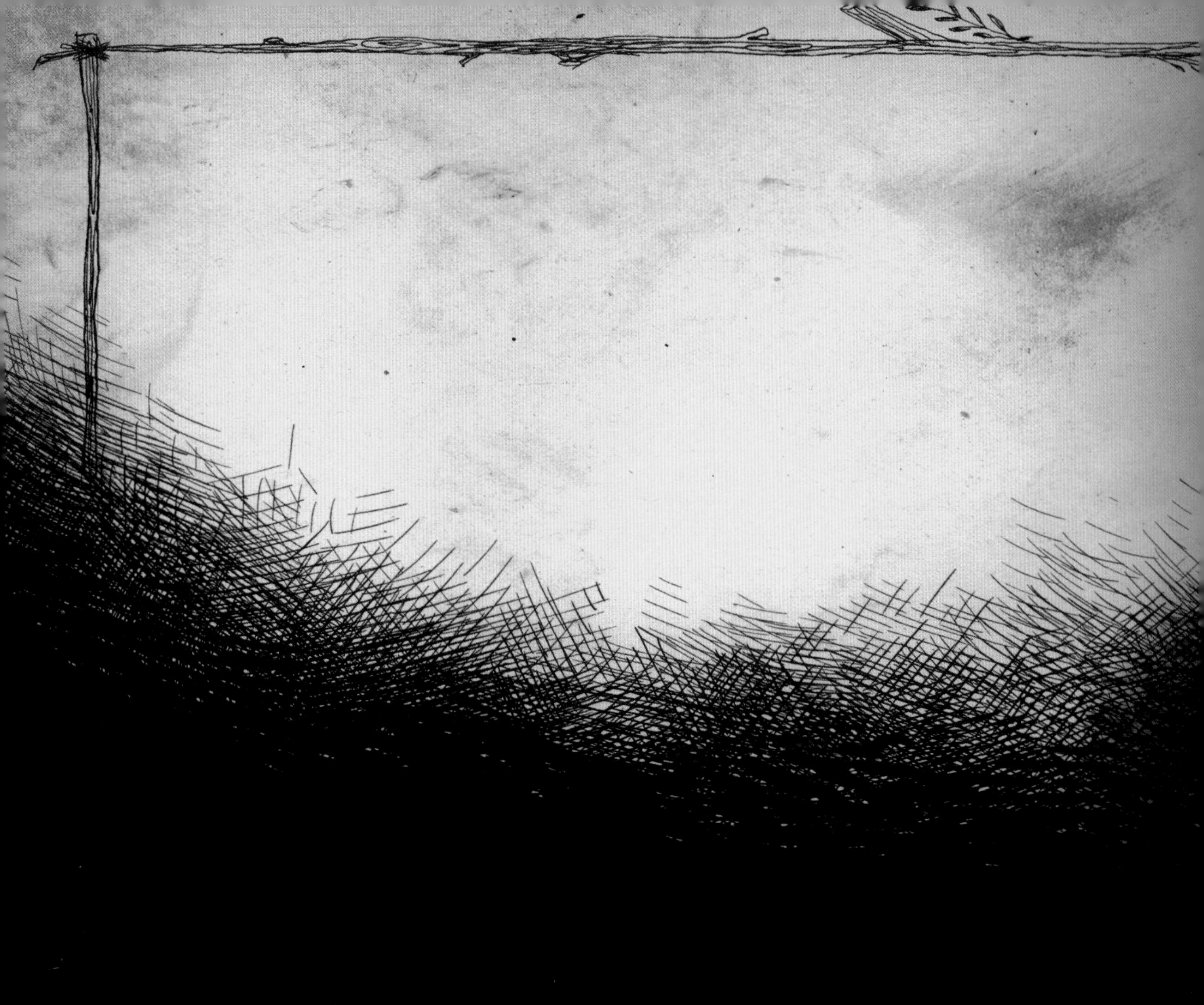

The music gets louder and louder, louder and louder. It is too much! The world is spinning! She feels like she is falling into the black spots of a leopard in the jungle!

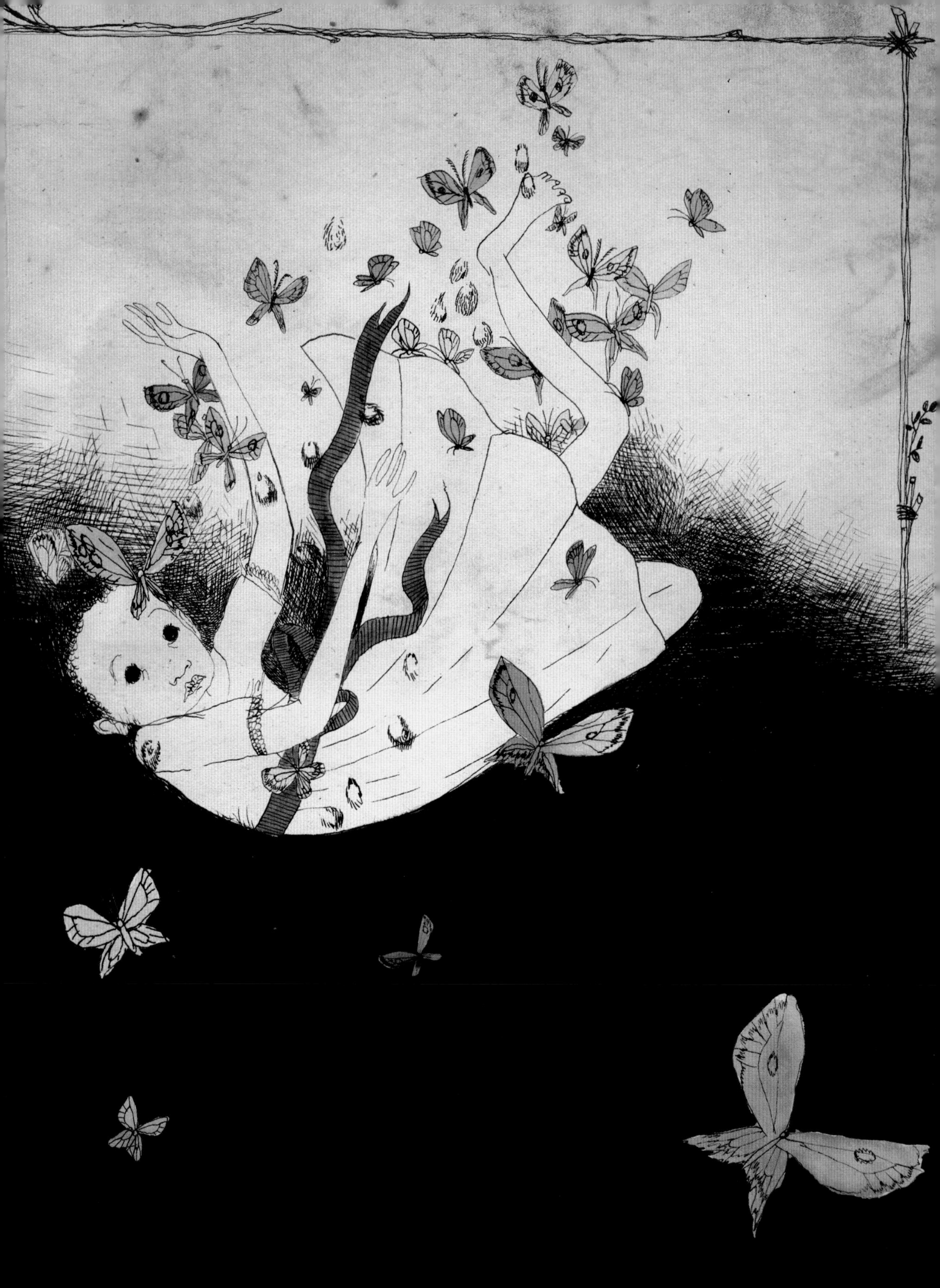

There go Blessing and Doubt, the sisters.

They walk out of the village on the muddy road.

The Gule Wamkulu are coming! They come out of the graveyard and creep through the cornfield!

Look out Blessing! Look out Doubt!

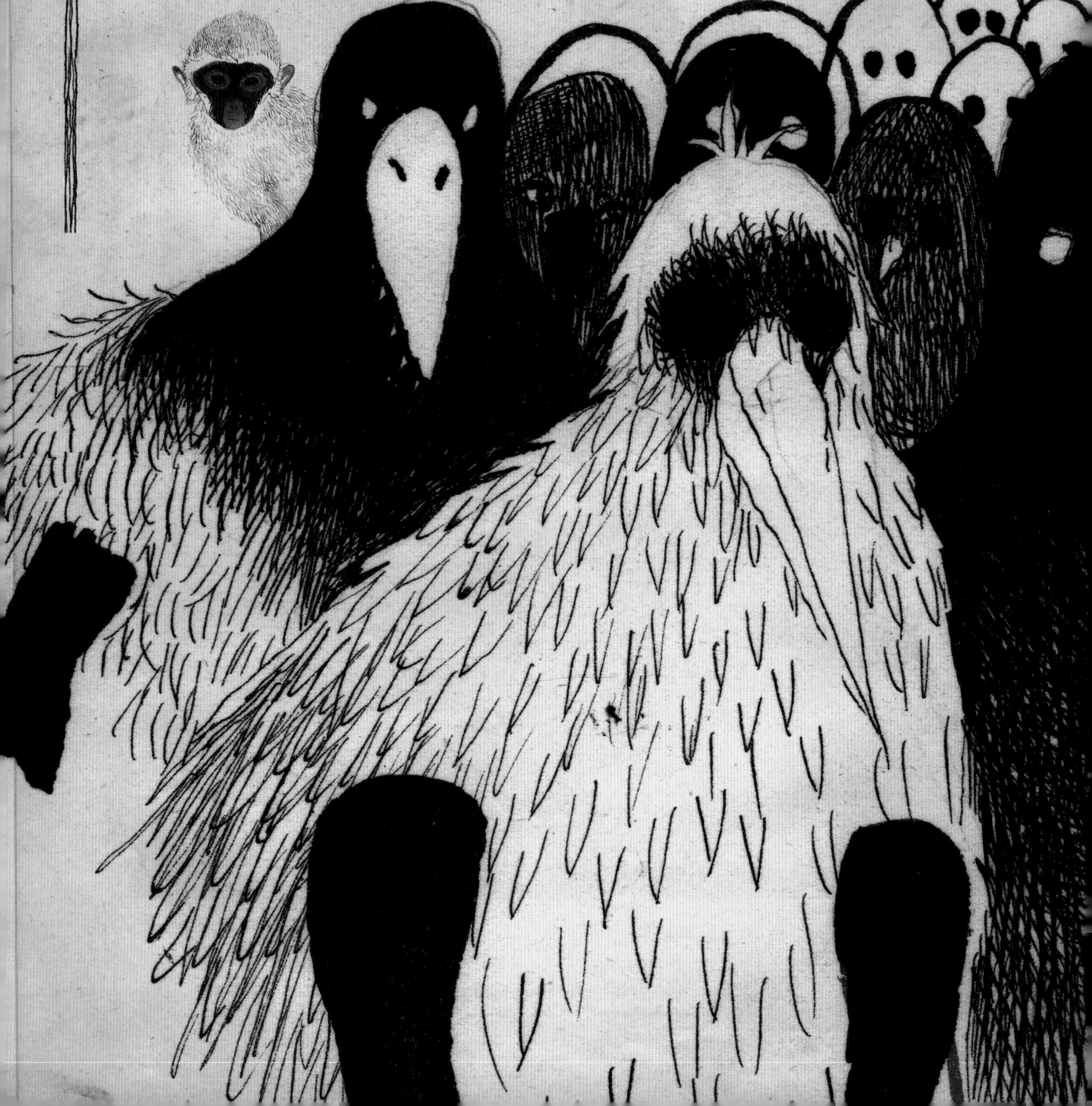

They carry Doubt away!
I would shout but it would set
the top of every tree on fire.

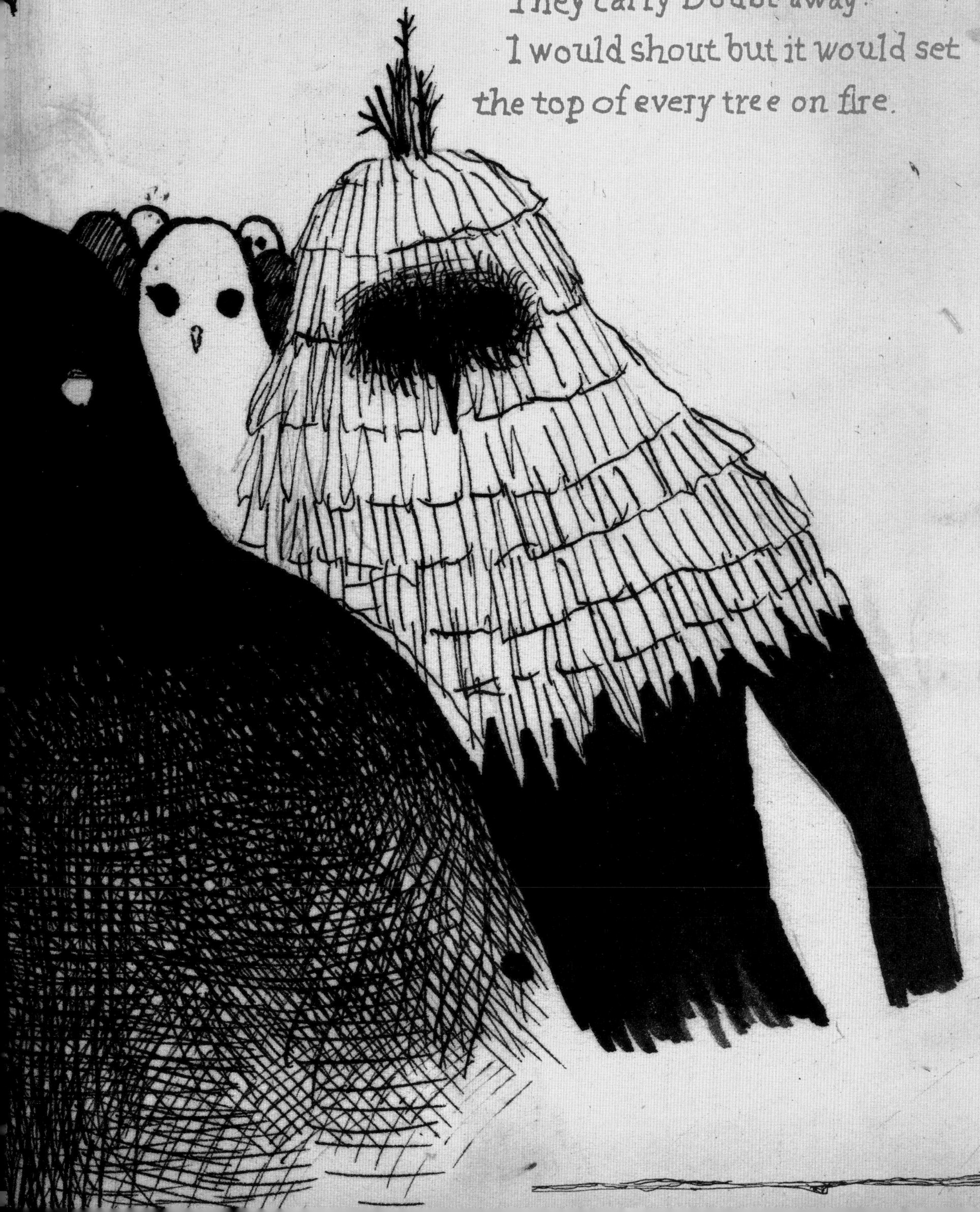

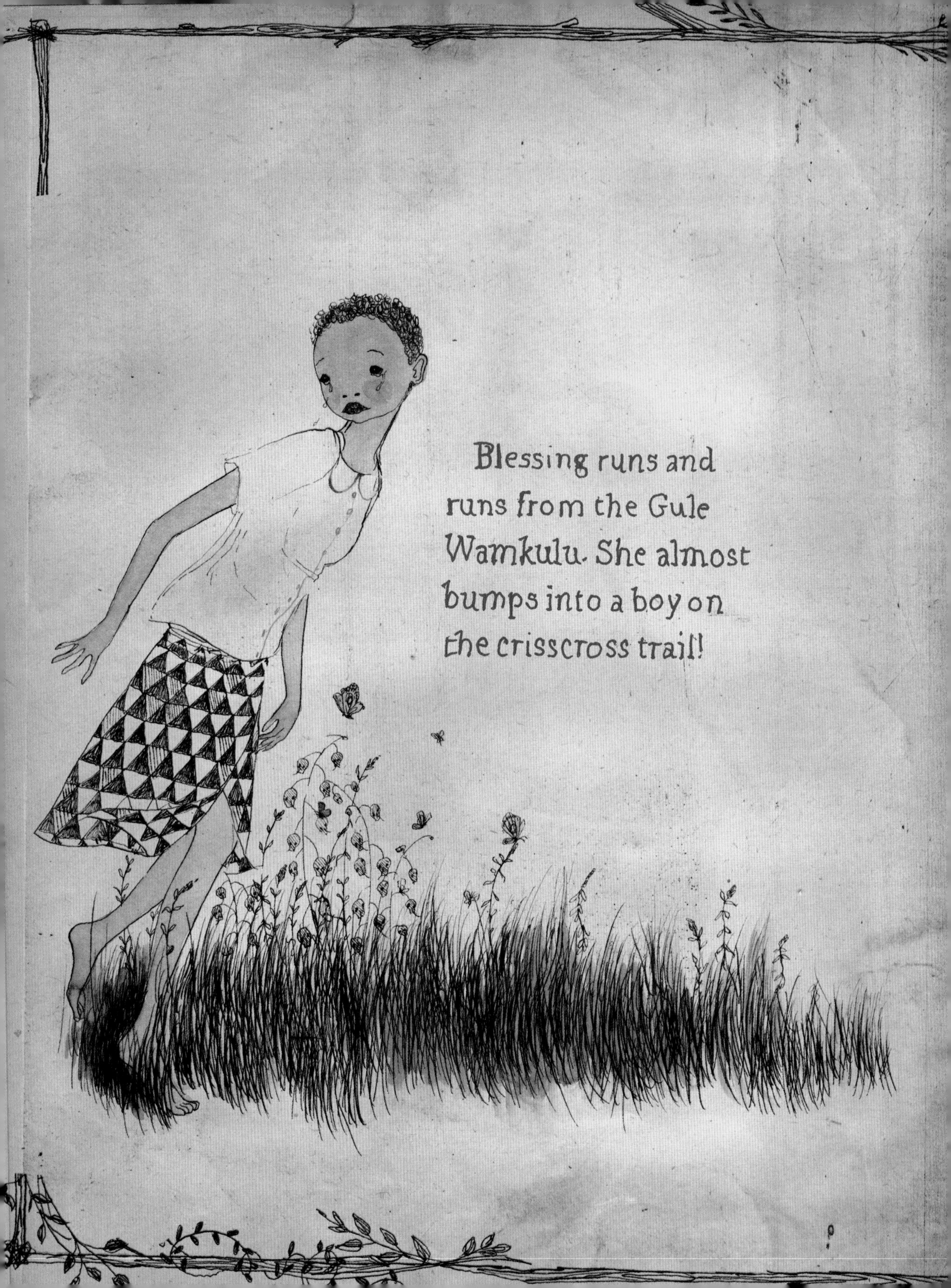

Blessing runs and runs from the Gule Wamkulu. She almost bumps into a boy on the crisscross trail!

Who is this boy? His name is Topher. He is an orphan too. He lived with his grandmother until one day she died. Topher cried himself to sleep! Then he dreamed that he should dig a hole in the anthill in the yard. He woke up and started digging. He dug a big hole.

He found a beautiful blue gemstone! The color of a dog's eye! No one had ever seen anything like it. Topher is going to the city to sell the stone to the gem cutter.

~Hello~ says Blessing.
~Hello~ says Topher.

But Ali Baba will see the baby! He closes
shop early and walks through the market. He
sees a man drop a cassava root!

A cassava root! Mmm!

Ali Baba looks left. He looks right. He picks
up the cassava root. It will be a big dinner!
~Stop thief! ~ shouts the man.
~Stop thief! ~ shout the police.
Ali Baba is going to jail!

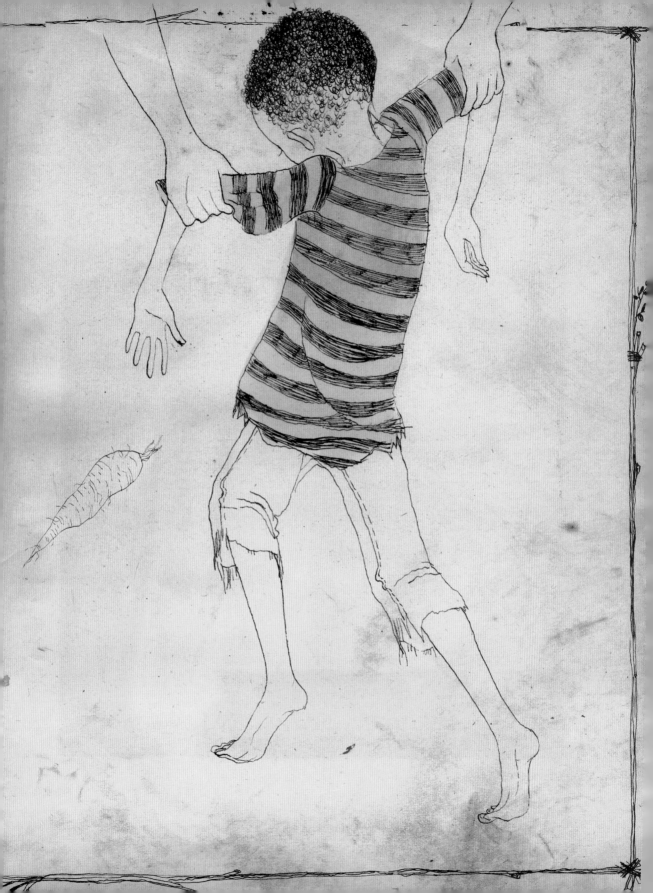

Oscar pedals the bicycle ambulance. He turns and turns and turns again. Everywhere he goes leaves and branches block the roadway. They mark the routes of funerals. It is Saturday, and there are funerals everywhere!

The wasting disease?

Yes, the wasting disease.

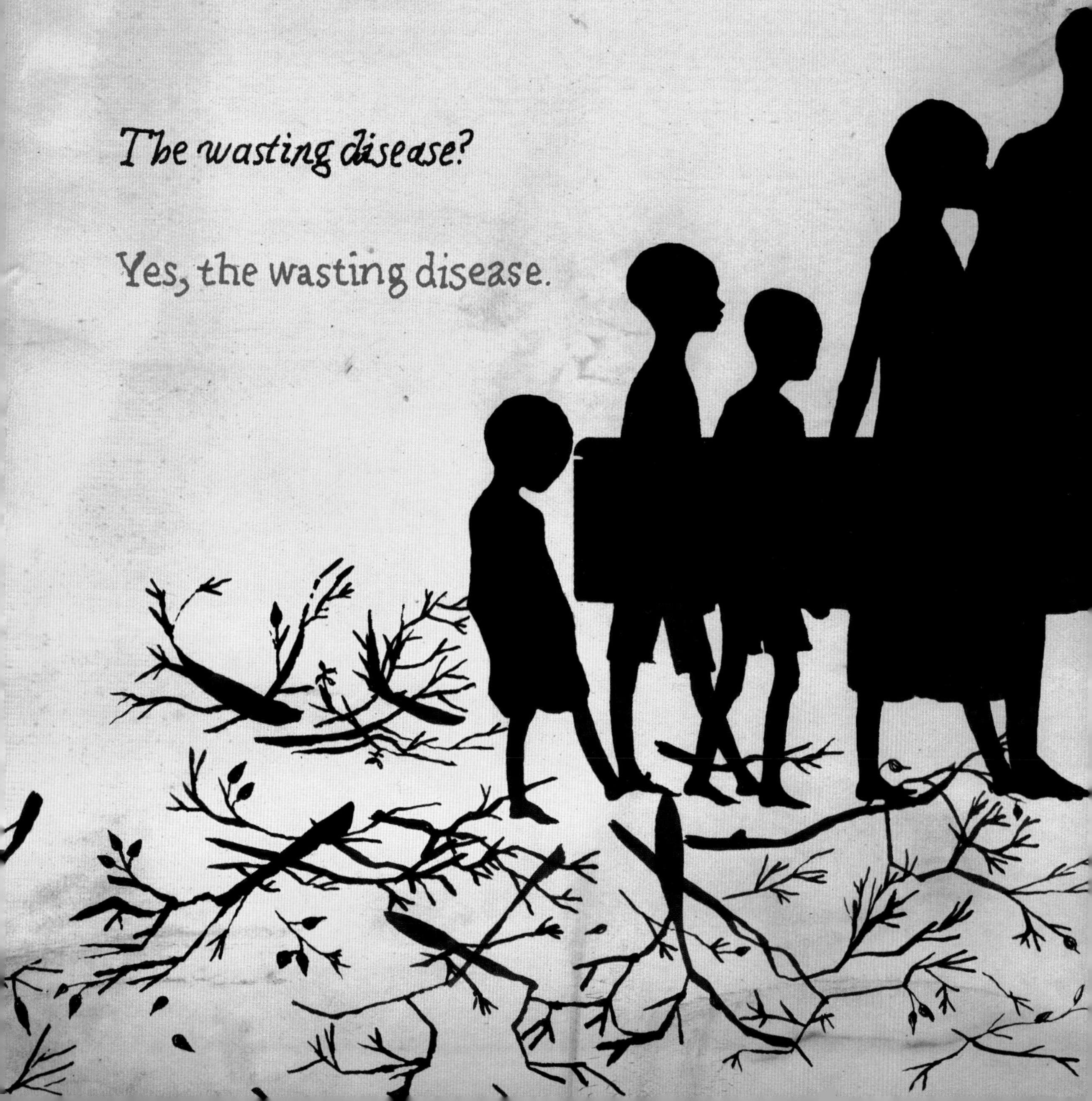

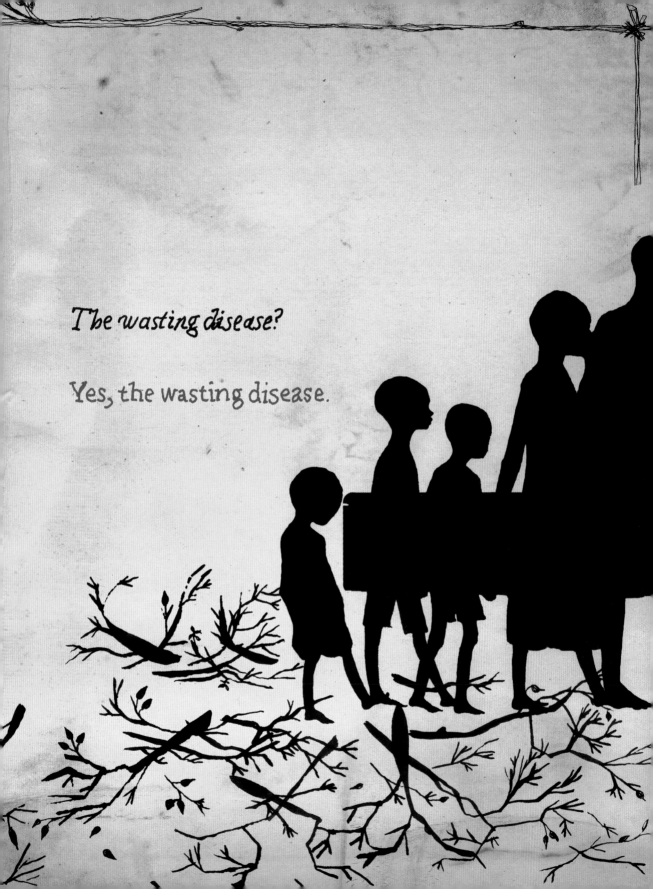

Look at Sugar! He is wearing his best suit. He has nine more coffins to build, but he wants to see the new baby!

There is someone at the door!

~An important man has died~ says the man at the door.
~He will need a coffin.~

~I already have nine coffins to build~ says Sugar.

~Ah!~ says the man. ~But this man will need your best coffin! An important man doesn't die very often. It is hard for a rich man to die!~

Now Sugar has ten coffins to build!

~Get to work!~ says the man.

What about Gift? Will she make it to see Mama?

She wakes up in a strange place.

The house is like a mushroom growing in a garden.

The roof is the color of mud. The walls go this way and that. Everything is covered in herbs and vines. Flowers rain down from the trees. Listen to the insects thrumming and zinging!

The sing'anga lives here. She is old!

~You are safe~ she says to Gift.

~I had a dream~ says Gift. ~I dreamed of a root that is shaped like a heart.~

~We will look for the root~ says the old woman.

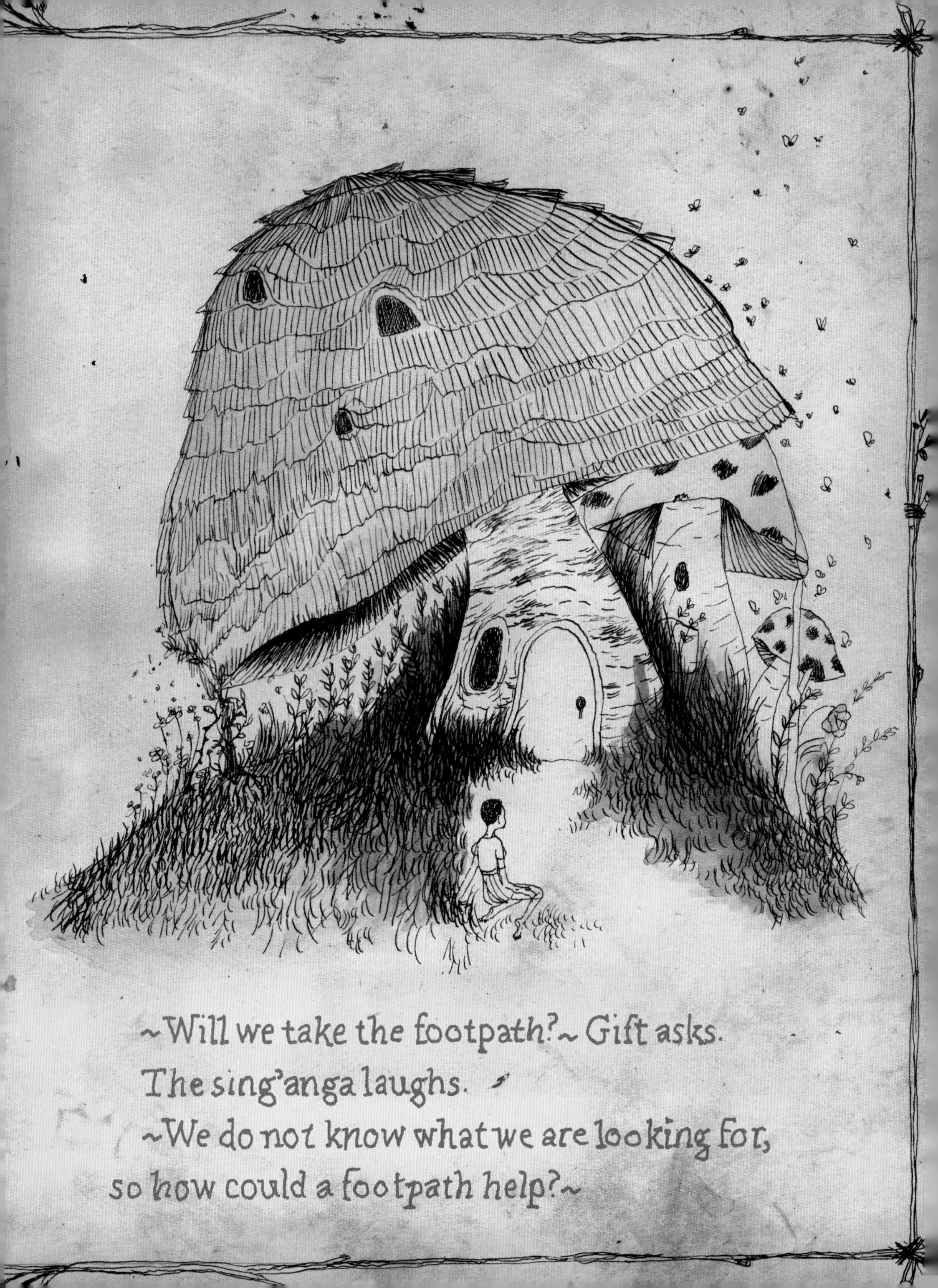

~Will we take the footpath?~ Gift asks.
The sing'anga laughs.
~We do not know what we are looking for,
so how could a footpath help?~

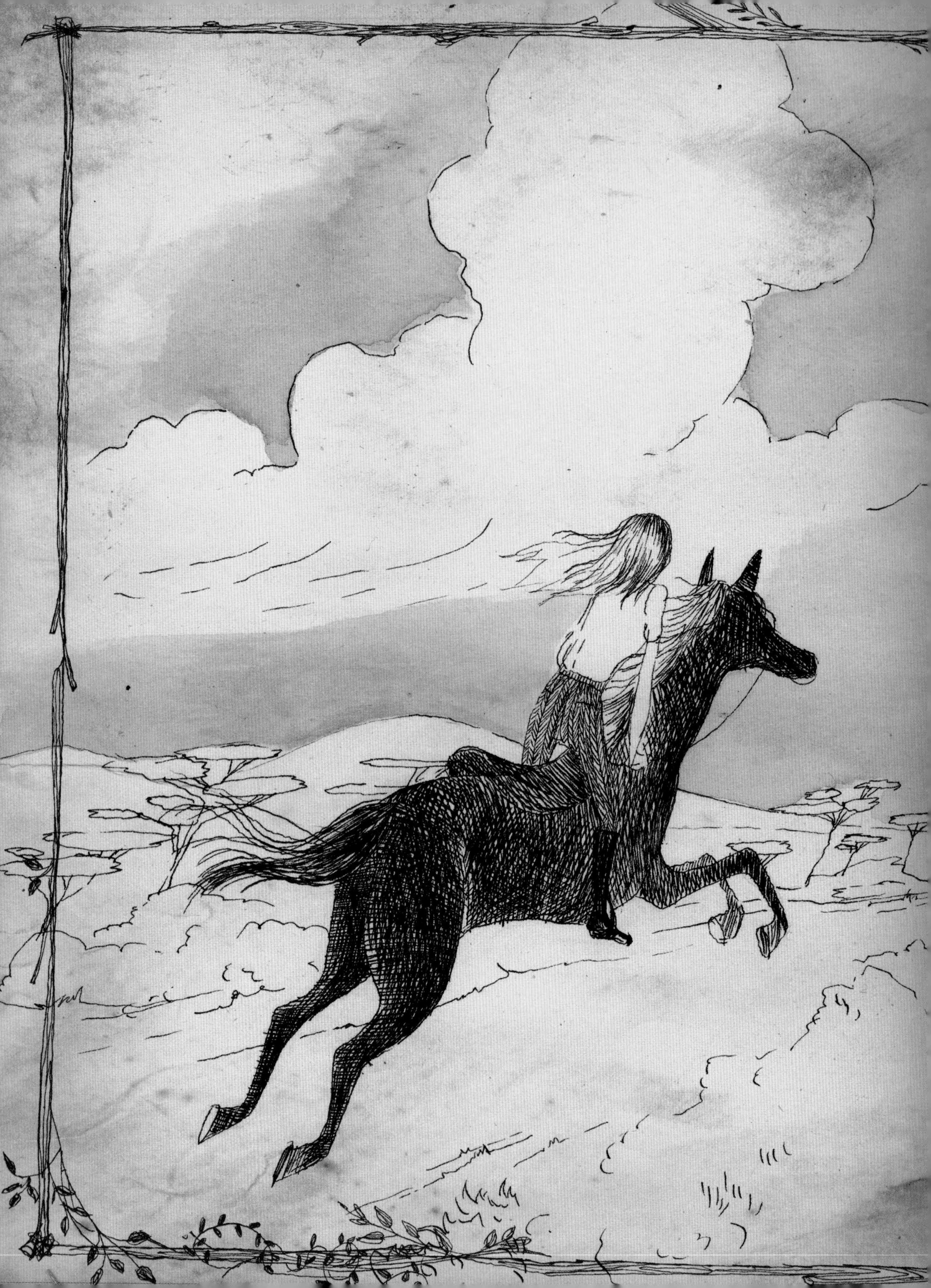

Who is left to see the baby? Only Krystal and Blessing and Lazarus!
　Well, Krystal will go to see Mama!
　She rides and she rides. She even jumps over a python!
　Then she sees her friends.
　~We are having a party!~ they say.

They are always having a party!

　~You must come! You must come! It will be the best party of the year!~

It is always the best party of the year!

　~Yes~ says Krystal. ~I will go to the party. I can see the new baby another day.~

Is Blessing coming to see Mama and the baby?
Ah, but Blessing has fallen in love.
Topher shows her the blue gemstone.
~I will find a thousand more!~ he says.
Blessing licks the air. She never makes up her mind without tasting the air.
~Yes~ she says. ~I will marry you~
It is the most beautiful story!

Maybe Lazarus will make it?

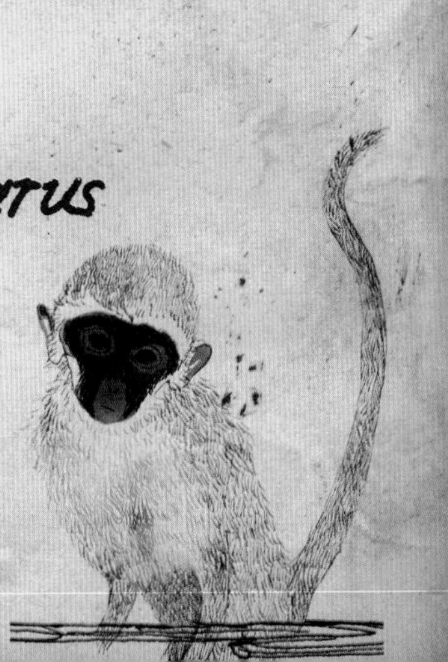

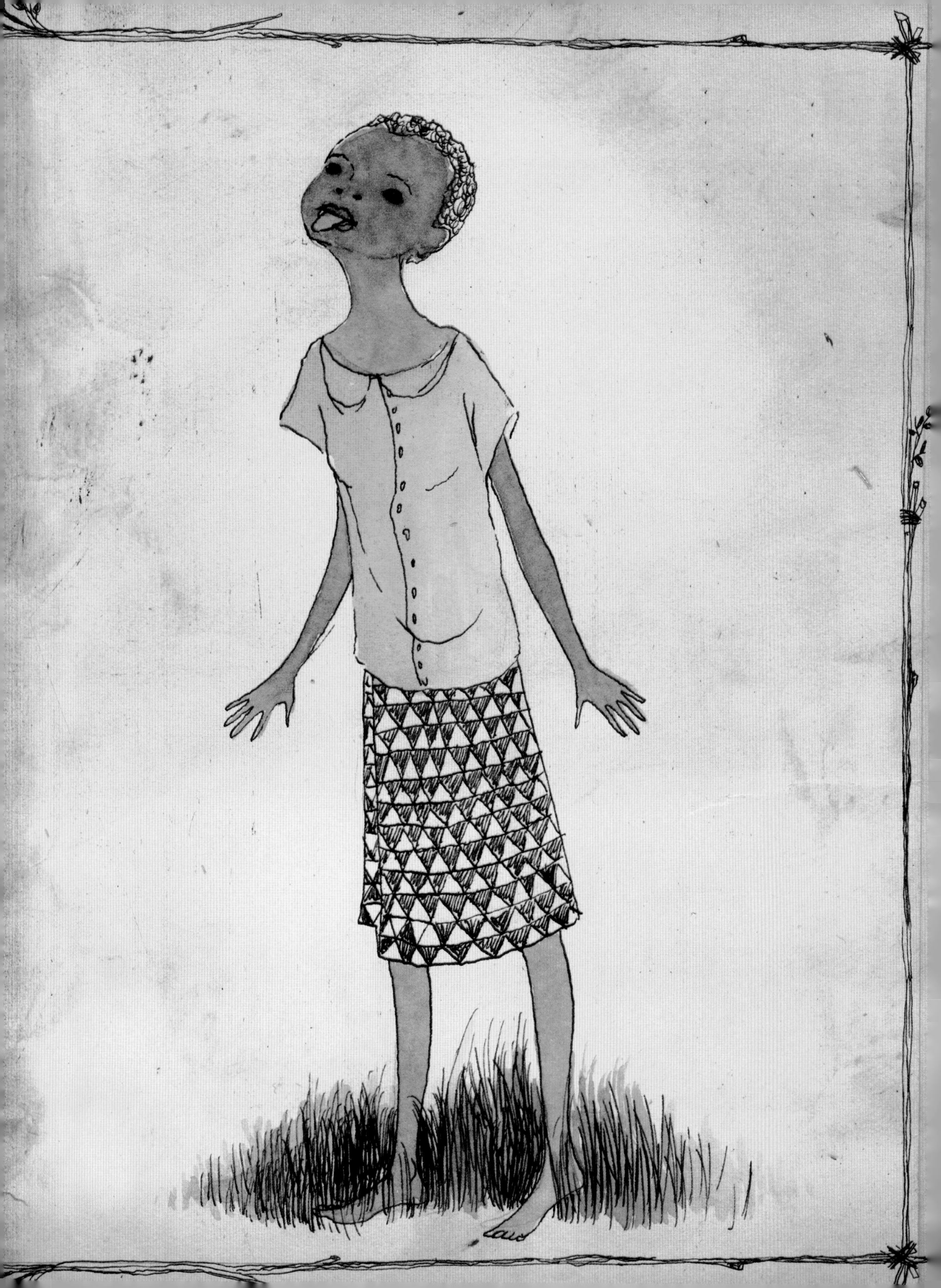

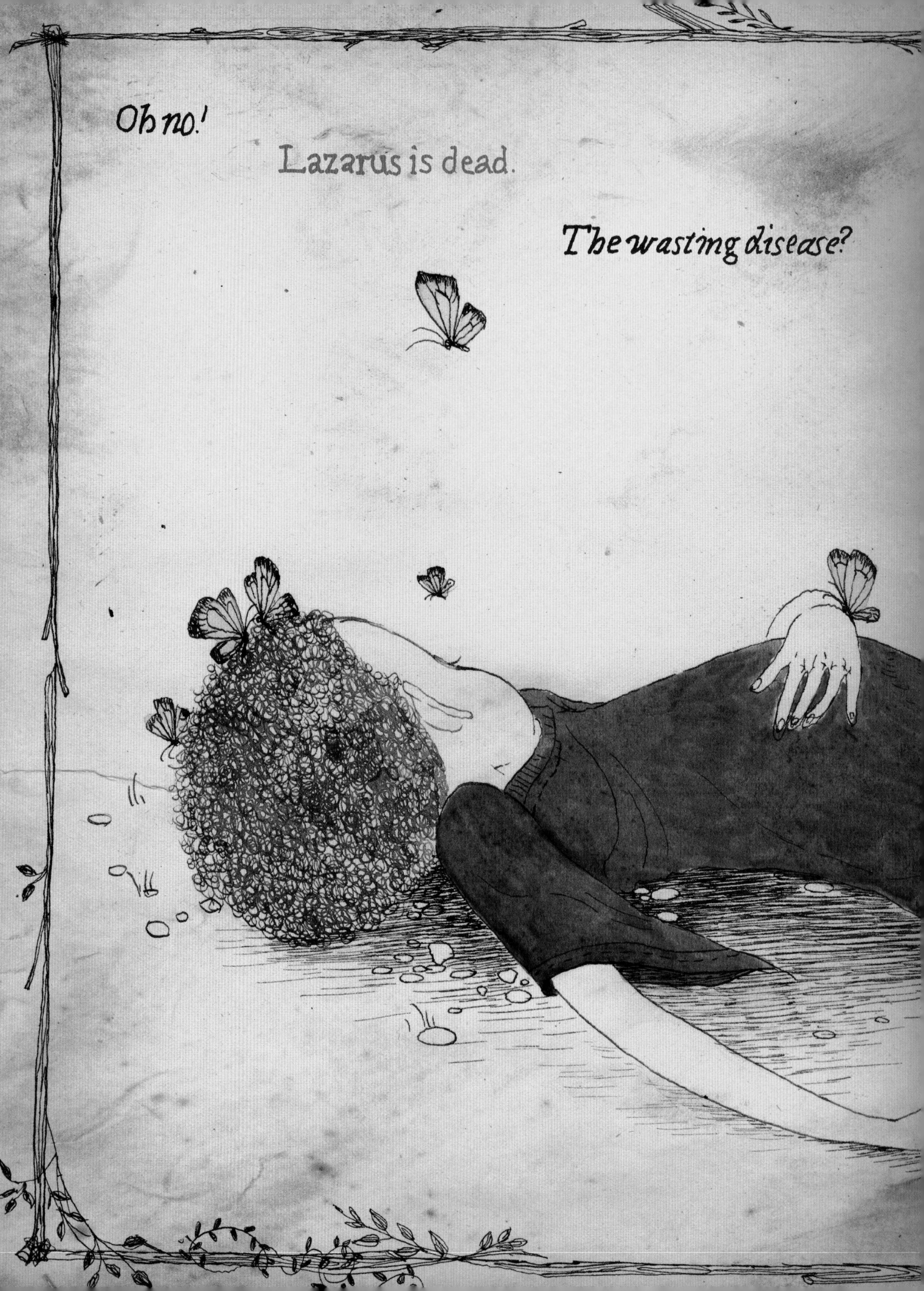
Oh no!
Lazarus is dead.
The wasting disease?

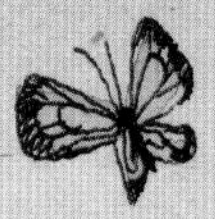

No. He was just too hungry.

I would cry but it would wash every person into the lake.

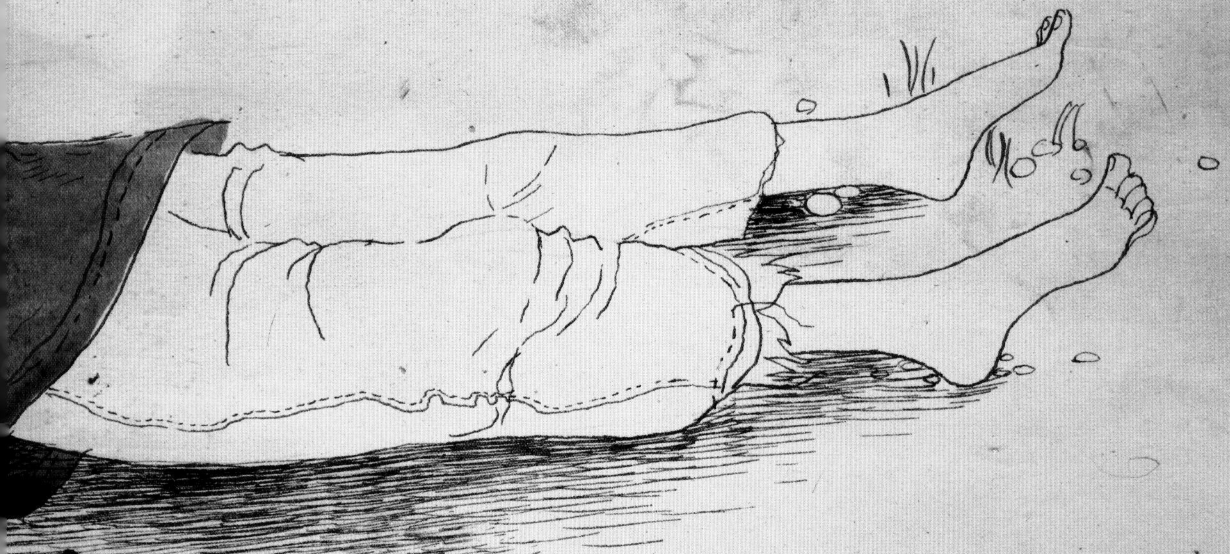

~Stop the bicycle!~ says Mama. ~Stop the bicycle right now!~

Oscar stops the bicycle. The baby is going to arrive!

I would cheer but it would scare every snake out of its hiding place.

Oscar and Mama look around. They
need to find a quiet place. Somewhere cool.
Somewhere green. Somewhere to welcome a
baby into the world!

  There is no time to think. There is only
one place!

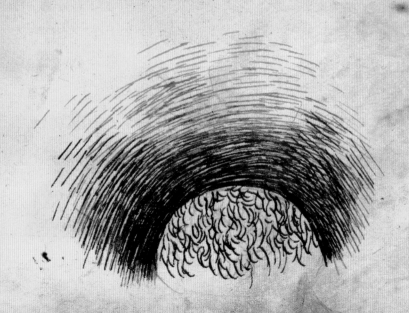

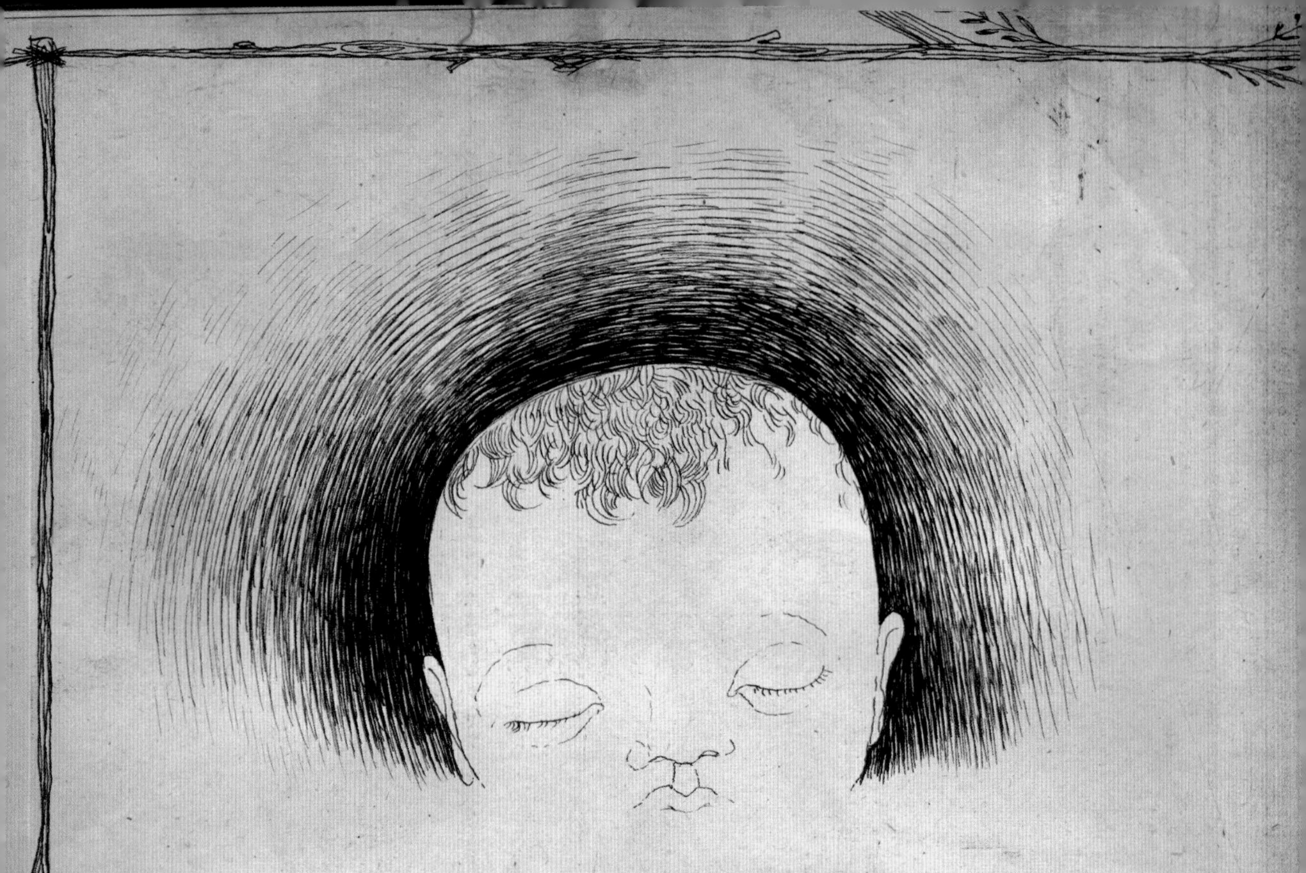

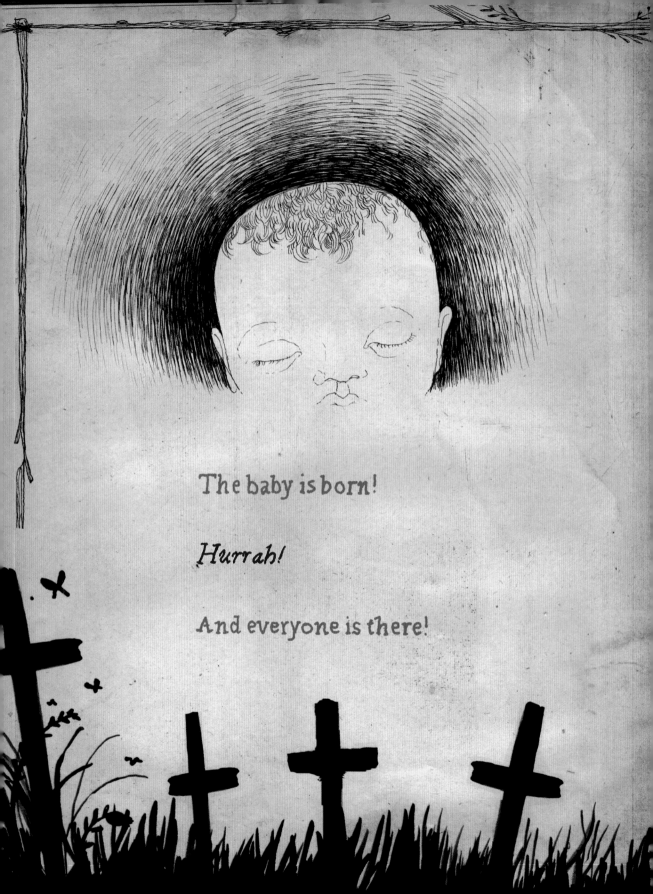

The baby is born!

Hurrah!

And everyone is there!

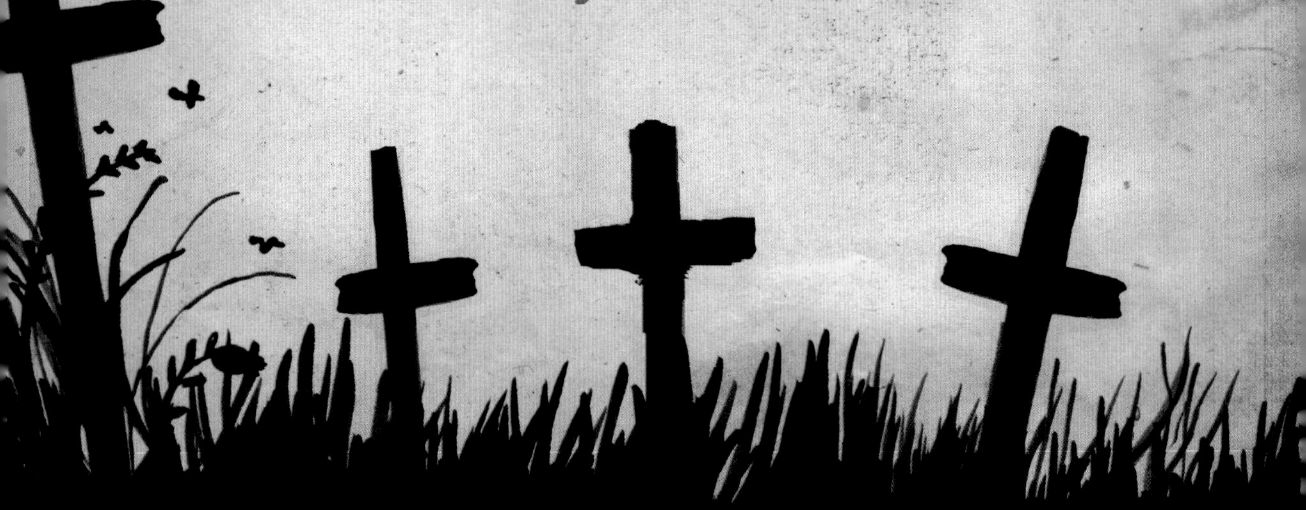

Where the raintree gives the sunset a sweet, sweet smell...
Where the hippos dance beneath the green lightning...
Where the fireflies follow you home...

Where Hope is born in a graveyard.

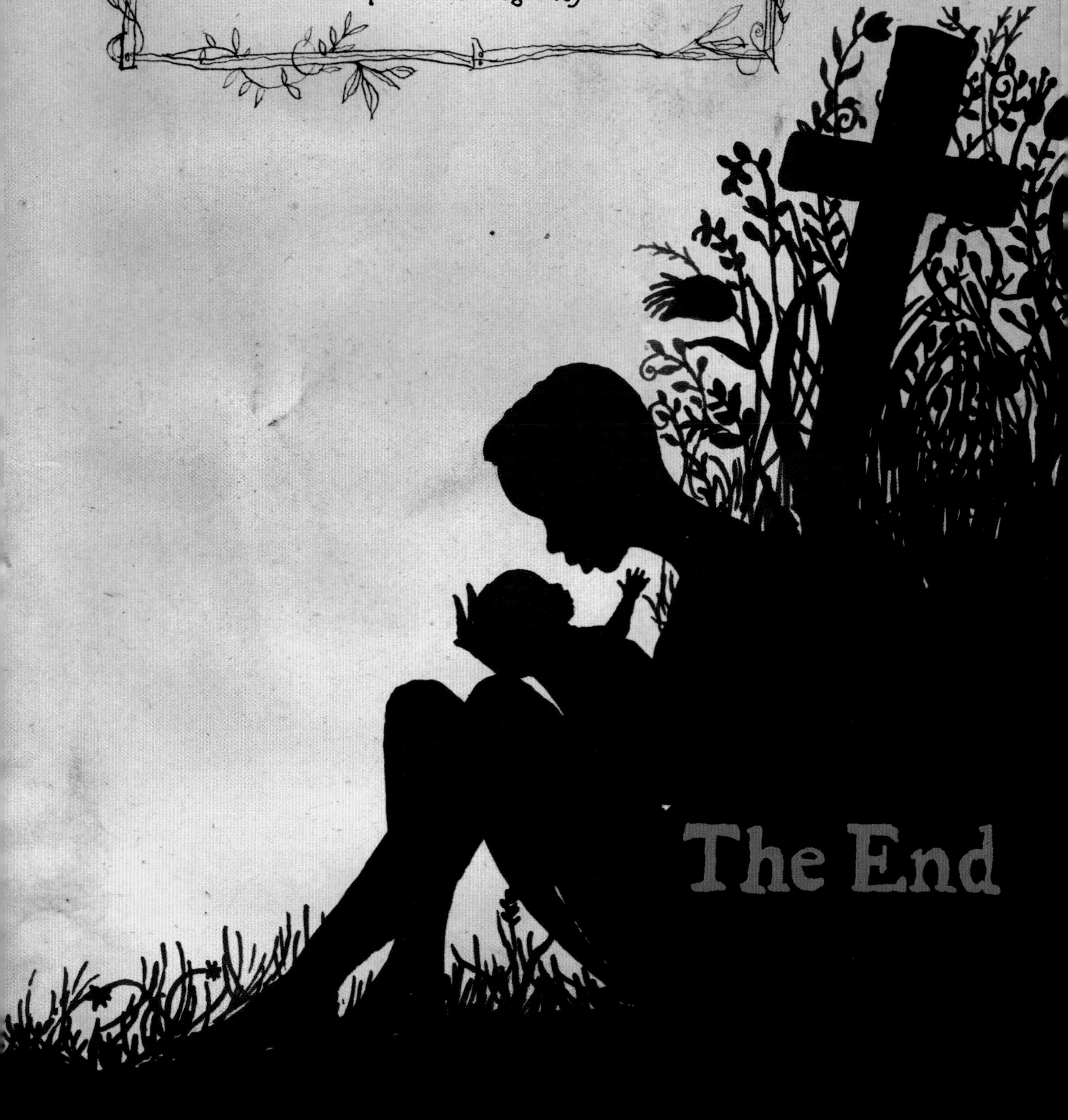

The End

Miriam Miriam

Miriam found me.

On the fourth day of nonstop meetings and presentations, I walked away. We were at a medical clinic, about to meet a girl in the final stages of AIDS. People were saying she could die that week, or even that day. Shouldn't dying be private?

My feet carried me out of the hospital in a rush, the kind where you don't think, you just move, and everything around you becomes a blur. I left the clinic and started walking the road out of town, the one nicknamed the AIDS superhighway because the disease travels with truckers and migrant workers and spreads in roadside brothels.

I don't know how long I walked. I had no map, mobile phone, or money. I'd left it all in the car.

So stupid.

I saw a gas station in the distance. Moving closer, I saw that it was guarded by a sweaty man, his bloodshot eyes staring down at his pump-action shotgun. Next to the gas station was a small store. I stepped inside, watching the truckers watch me while they paid for beer and chips. I started to explain that I was lost, I needed help.

"Excuse me, miss, you could use my phone."

I turned to see a girl in a tan uniform – an employee from the gas station. Her long braids were tied back and she had full red lips.

"I'm Miriam. It's okay now."

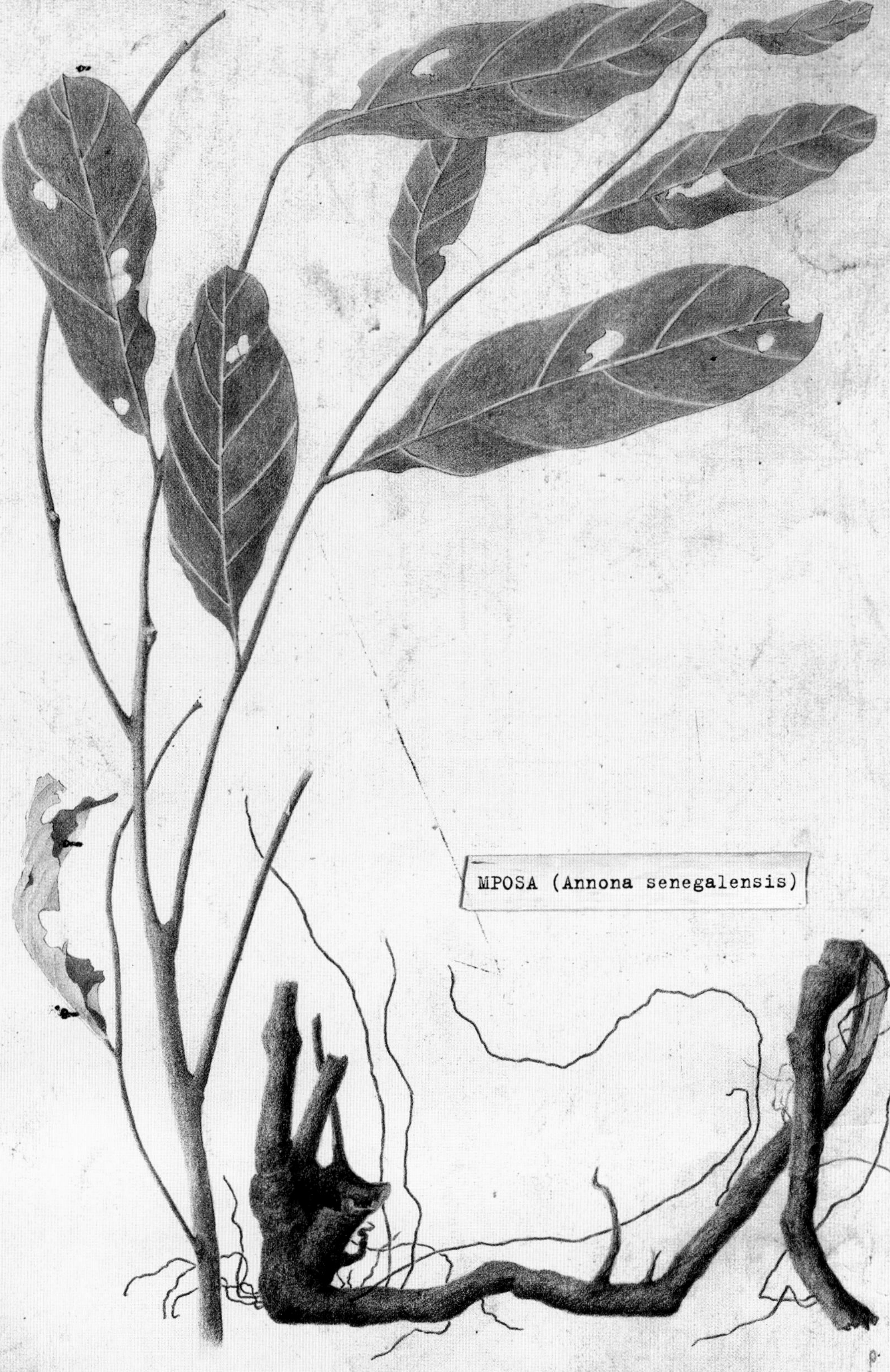

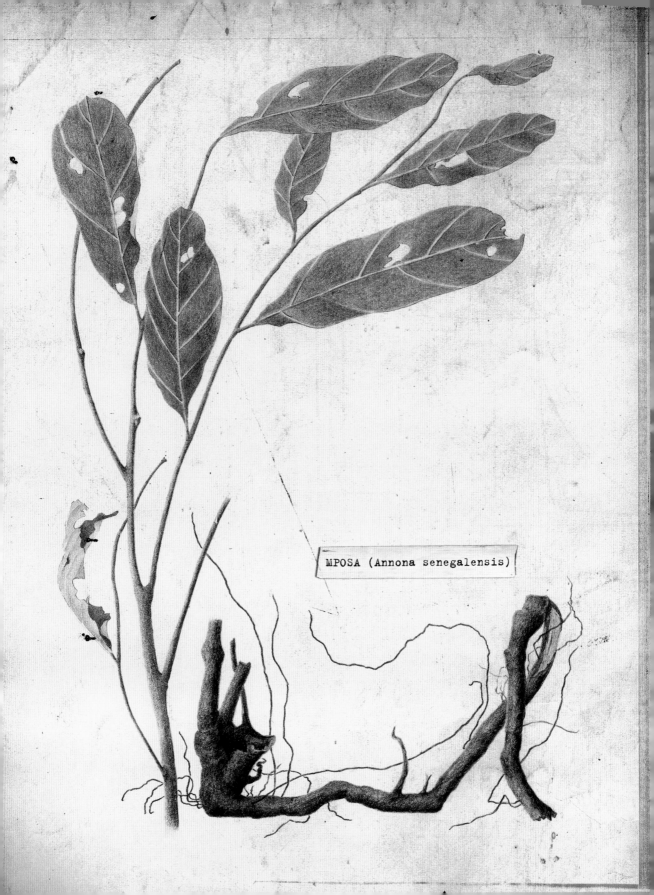

MPOSA (Annona senegalensis)

Days later I am sitting in her bedroom. Being with Miriam is like standing in the warm sun after you've taken a swim in an icy ocean.

She likes to take my hand, and throws her head back when she laughs with this giant belly laugh. She peppers her sentences with "God bless" and "thank God." Her head tilts upward when she talks, dignified, and when she looks at me, she does so with piercing kindness.

"I am one of them," Miriam had whispered to me quickly at the gas station.

"One of what?"

"Those people with the AIDS."

Miriam comes from a middle-class family. Her spoken English is perfect. Outside her window is her family's maize field, perfect stalks of corn following the sun. Her bed has no mattress — instead, thick wool blankets cover rusted springs. There is paint on the wall but most of it has peeled off.

Miriam's story begins with a man, Rexious. She becomes pregnant. They decide to marry, but then he runs away. It is Miriam's sister who learns that Rexious also has another wife, in a different township, also pregnant — and that this other girl is very sick.

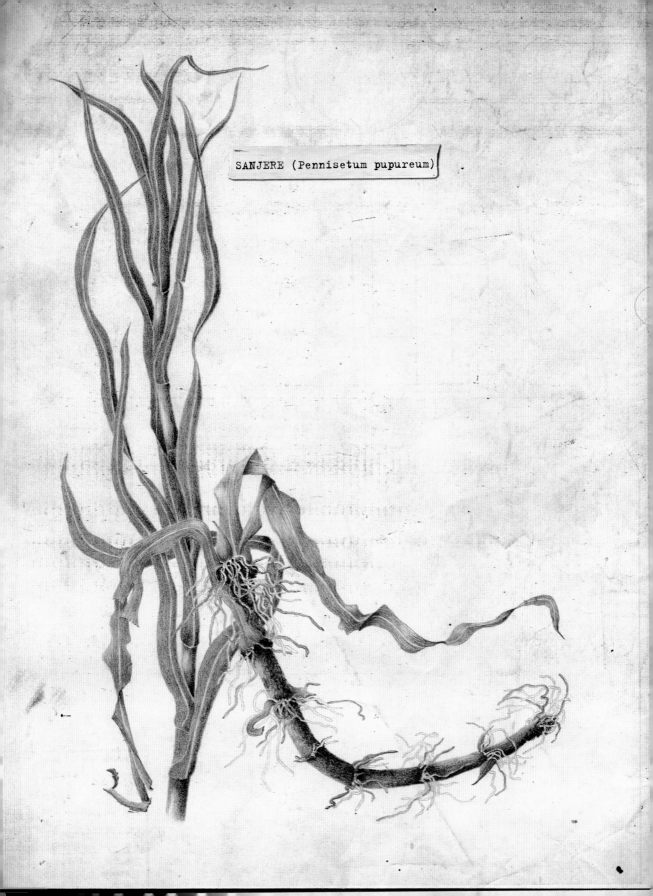

SANJERE (Pennisetum pupureum)

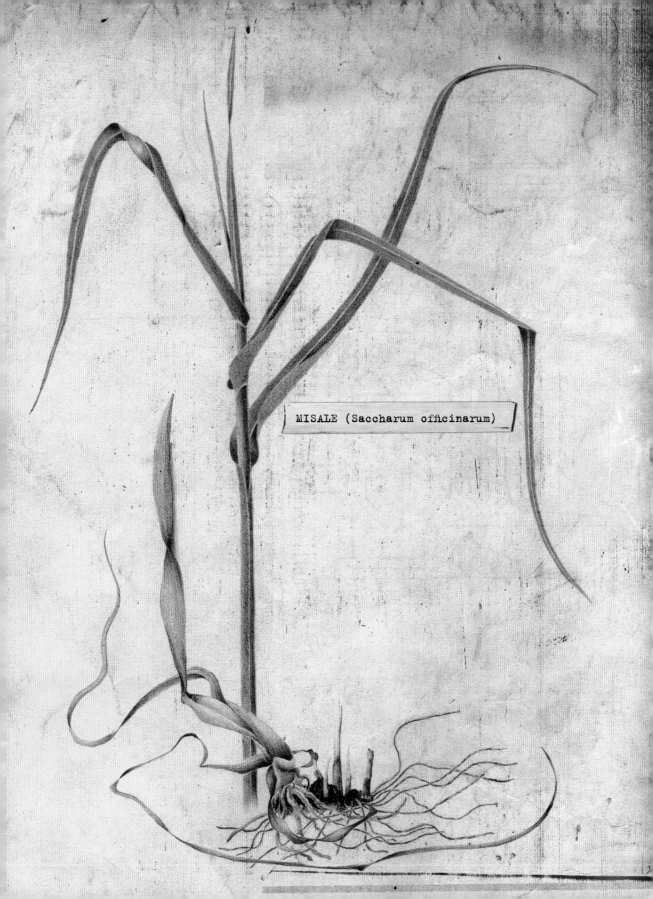

MISALE (Saccharum officinarum)

By the time Miriam is eight months pregnant, she has sores all over her vagina. When it is time to deliver her child, the doctors tell her the sores will prevent a safe birth. "My vagina is cut open instead," she says. On April 18, her baby is born. Miriam cannot walk, but her mother takes care of her. "She even washes me down there." Miriam names her daughter Sunshine - the little one is sick all the time, but the family does its best. Miriam must return to work and help support the family.

She pumps gas seven days a week. The fumes give her headaches - even Panadol doesn't help. Miriam finds herself at the African Bible Hospital, where they ask if they can test her for AIDS. The medics draw her blood and ask her to wait just 15 minutes. She knows. It is just this feeling that comes over her, heavy and dense. When they call her back into the office she can hear the nurse speaking, but more so she can feel her own tears.

She doesn't normally cry, she says, and asks me if I know why tears are hot.

Miriam doesn't come from a family of weak people, so she just stops crying, like turning off a hose. She thanks the nurse for her time and straightens her skirt, brushing off the dust that had fallen on her dress. She would walk out of the hospital as though it were just another day.

There will be no more men in her life. She will never have sex again. She will never fall in love again. She will live with her parents and her daughter. As she tells me this, I can see Miriam imagining her life. She will go to work at 5:30 a.m., come home in the evening, play with Sunshine, and get up to start the same routine again and again. Her lids become heavy.

"I thank God for Sunshine. My best friend," says Miriam. The baby lies between Miriam and me, her hand reaching up toward her mother. Sunshine's nails are so tiny and perfectly cut. She's almost a year old. Miriam tells me that the local hospital has said that Sunshine is too young to be tested.

I had to tell her that it wasn't true.

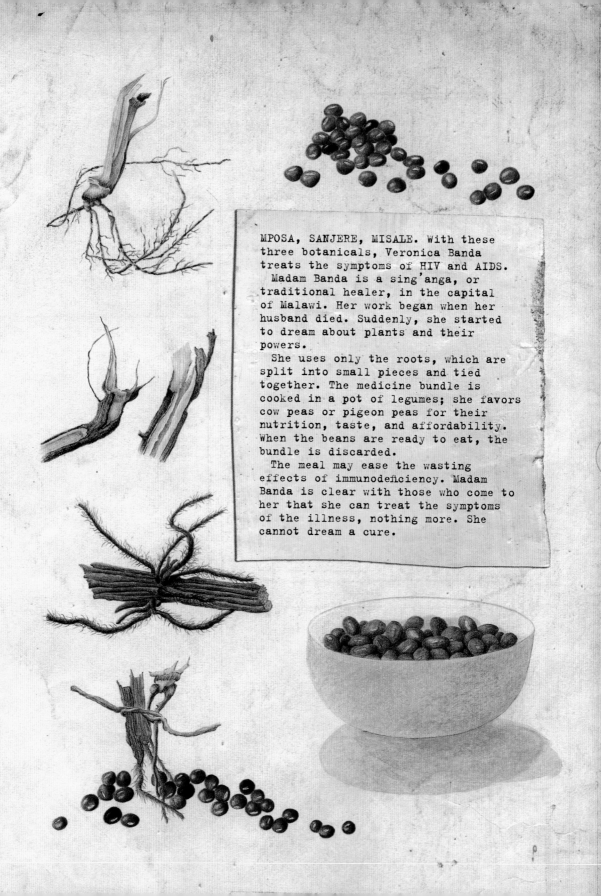

MPOSA, SANJERE, MISALE. With these
three botanicals, Veronica Banda
treats the symptoms of HIV and AIDS.

Madam Banda is a sing'anga, or
traditional healer, in the capital
of Malawi. Her work began when her
husband died. Suddenly, she started
to dream about plants and their
powers.

She uses only the roots, which are
split into small pieces and tied
together. The medicine bundle is
cooked in a pot of legumes; she favors
cow peas or pigeon peas for their
nutrition, taste, and affordability.
When the beans are ready to eat, the
bundle is discarded.

The meal may ease the wasting
effects of immunodeficiency. Madam
Banda is clear with those who come to
her that she can treat the symptoms
of the illness, nothing more. She
cannot dream a cure.

I am wishing so many things as I hold the phone.
   "Miriam? Did you hear back from the clinic?"
   I'm standing on the deck at the lodge. The day sits at the
edge of dusk, and cicadas trill in the forest. The whole lodge
feels like it's vibrating, even floating. The guests around me are
served their evening cocktails. "You can't find reverse gear
in this country," says one, loudly retelling a joke to a friend.
"That's because it's stuck in reverse gear. It's always going
backward."
   Over the phone I can hear diesel trucks and the staccato thud
of men's voices interrupting Miriam's breathing. She must be
back at work.
   "Miriam? Can you hear me?"
   "She has it," she says, drawing her breath in sharply.

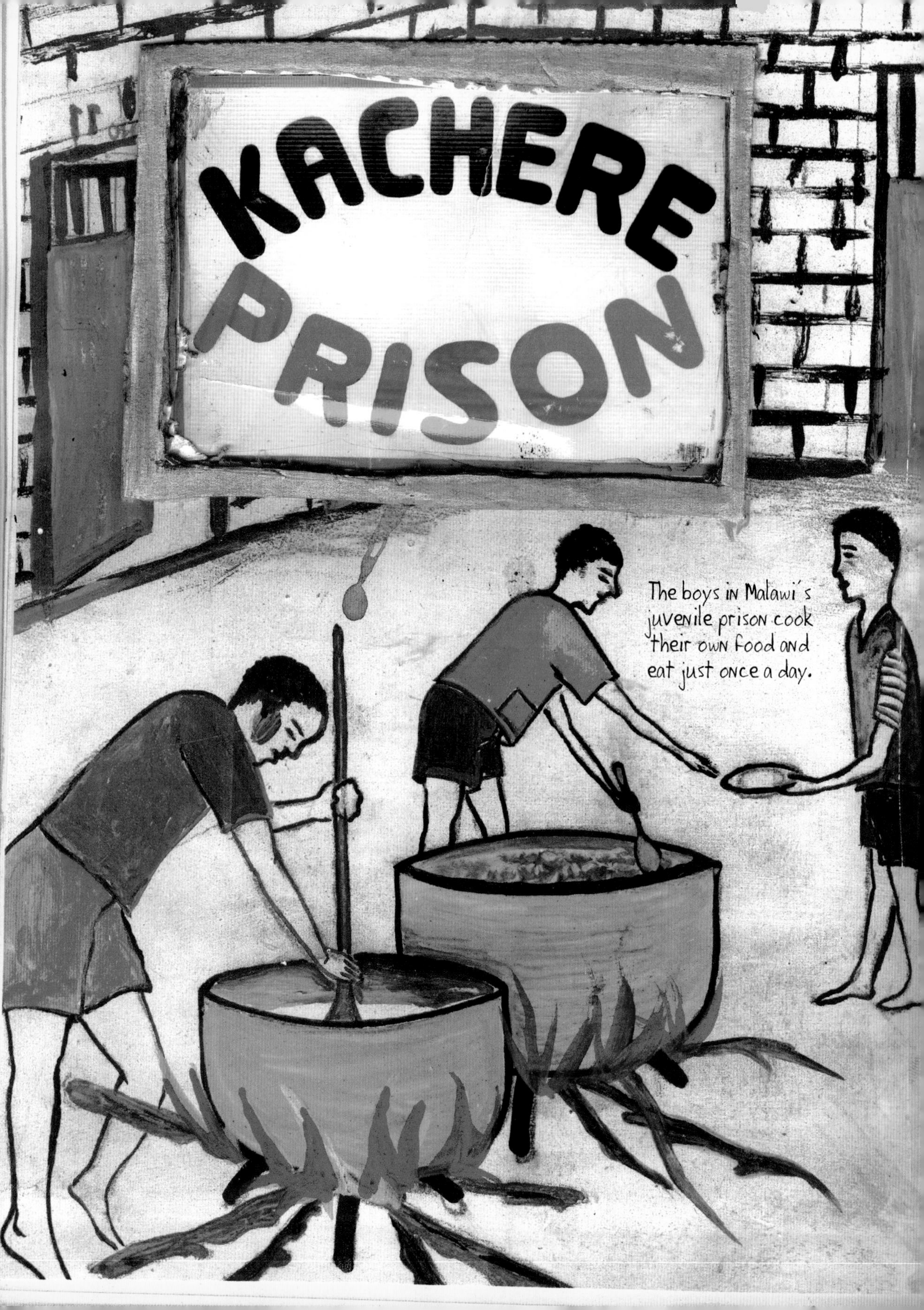
KACHERE
PRISON
The boys in Malawi's juvenile prison cook their own food and eat just once a day.

We are standing in a courtyard. Four white walls, the random balls of barbed wire on top more ceremonial than functional. There is an oversize cauldron on the far side of the yard. It must be where the cooking is done. Thick white smoke furls out from under the pot.

We have been allowed into Kachere prison, Lilongwe's jail for juveniles. It feels like sheer luck that we were ushered in - our local guide, Laws Chiunda, had officiated a marriage ceremony for one of the guards. Half-asleep in the midafternoon heat, the officer in charge found the key to the courtyard door and let us in. The whitewashed plaster was blinding.

Mr. Chiunda motions for me to stand in front of the boys as they count themselves off for roll call. There are 54 of them.

"They have come here to our country to teach you," the head guard tells the boys. "Let us thank God that they are here. Show them respect and say thank you as they hand you your gifts."

The boys are in perfect rows, like the Jaffa oranges in the wooden crates that my father would buy each year as the winter began. The boys sit upright - when flies or mosquitoes land in their eyelashes, they don't move. Most look away from me, shy, like they haven't been around a girl in a long time. They're between 11 and 19 years old. Most are in the awkward throes of puberty.

I have a bag of soap bars in my hand. I pull out the greasy blocks - acrid with the odor of animal fat. Some boys allow the sides of their hands to brush mine as they take the soap. Tips of fingers swollen like the heads of eggplants.

The juveniles were transferred to Kachere a year ago. Prior to that, they'd been housed with adults. Rape was common in these

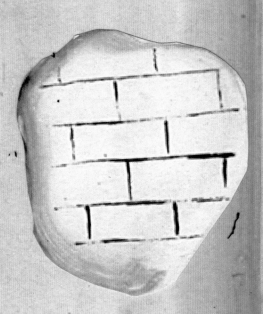

Fifty percent of
Kachere's inmates
are orphans, and 50
percent are waiting
for trial - or even
for charges.

prisons - boys, the easy targets of men. After a <u>New York Times</u> article was published about prison conditions in Malawi, the boys were quietly shuffled to the current facility.

Their feet are bare. I can't see any shoes in the yard. In fact, there is nothing except the giant cauldron. This is where the boys stay all day, following slim bands of shade along the white walls. Their curly hair is red-tipped, bleached by malnutrition and constant exposure to the sun. Beads of sweat move down some boys' shining skin - malarial fevers? Shredded shirts slide off of tiny shoulders, dark stains on their tattered shorts. They start to cough. As one boy coughs, so does another, then another.

The head guard is looking toward me to introduce myself. It feels as though I need to say just the right thing to be allowed back in tomorrow. I can't concentrate. I'm too nervous. I tell the boys that I like to read and listen to music and ride my bike. I'm thinking that I should be afraid, they are prisoners, and prisons are violent places. They just look like little boys.

Most of these kids are in here for some minor crime like stealing maize or a mobile phone, or illegally selling minibus tickets. Some are in for rape and murder. All of these boys are poor. And here's the catch: No one really wants to keep most of these boys in prison. If there was someone to post their bail, they could walk free. But they are orphans, or their families are too poor or too far away. They're trapped. Set them free and they have nowhere to go and nothing to do - they will only steal again, or get caught up in other crimes.

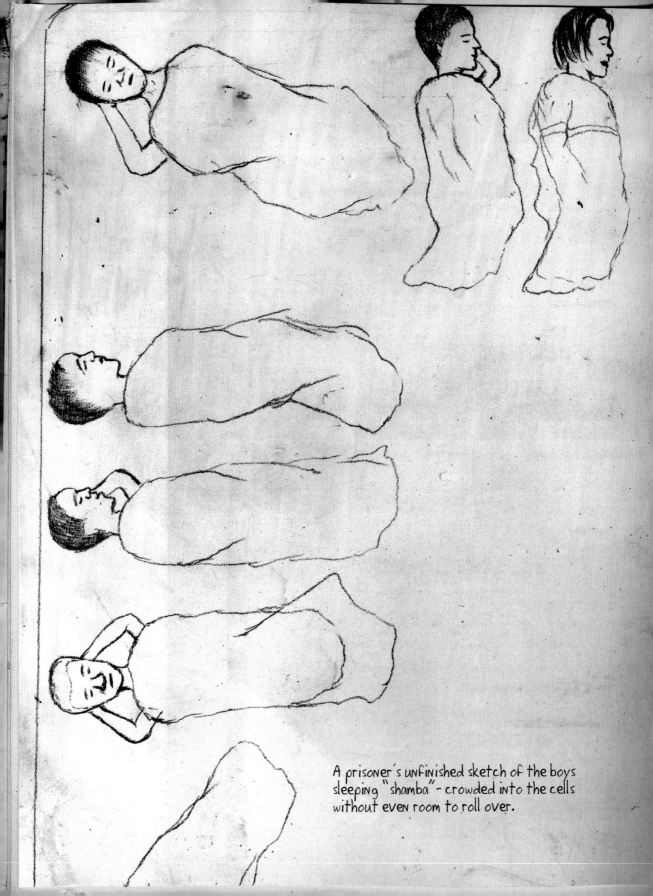

A prisoner's unfinished sketch of the boys sleeping "shamba" – crowded into the cells without even room to roll over.

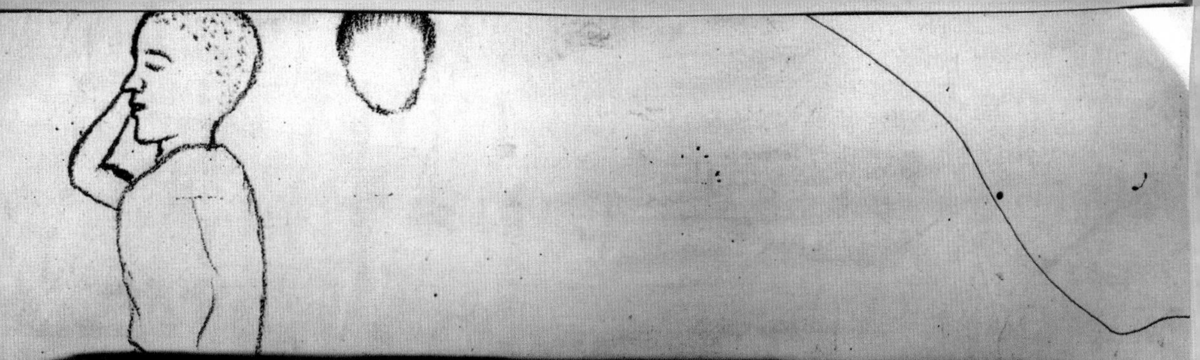

So where do you start? Where do you focus the resources of one of the planet's poorest countries? Do you take care of the HIV/AIDS first? What about the tuberculosis or the cholera? Do you start with the starvation, or the illnesses that make people too weak to raise their own crops? This generation's orphans, or the next generation of parents who might die from AIDS? It's dizzying, the strain this country is under.

The guards look haggard and thin. They don't carry guns and some don't even have batons. The way the guards look at the boys - it's not what I expected. Their smiles are almost paternal, weary and tender. The officer in charge keeps a list of what he needs to improve Kachere: bags of cement for a proper kitchen, toilets and showers that work, sewing machines, electricity in the cells, blankets, water buckets, plates, uniforms, exercise books, textbooks, pens for the boys. The guards, he said, live in staff housing not much better than prison chambers.

I've been wondering why the guards let us into Kachere, and then I realize: They want us here. They are risking their jobs because they want us to see. I blink back the sudden tears.

The boys are still sitting quietly under the sun, listening to the words that I barely know I'm saying.

"Do you have any questions for us?" I ask the boys.

This kid who looks about 12, precocious, stands up. "Can we have a ball?"

That's it?

That's all you want?

First receive my greetings. How are you? I am fine
if you are fine.

My fellow friends, take care here—there are
dangerous things. I am happy because of your
coming. God loves the world equally, so all we
people have to love each other.

But this prison is killing.

The aim of this letter is to explain why I am
here in Kachere Prison. I do business. I sell
roasted maize. As I was working at around past
ten o'clock I saw the policemen. I went to greet
them, then they told me that we want you and your
friend. So we have been found with a case of
stealing a cell phone. We were beaten to reveal
anything about the phone but we told them we did
not know anything.

You always have bad thoughts when you are being
accused of something you did not commit.

Why is it that you put a long sentence to the
person who has been convicted for the first time?

And who put the law that when one is wrong he
should be imprisoned and when did this law start
and which country did it start in?

I am asking you to help.

It is difficult for me to understand that I have no
one to support me.

My elder brother was beating my mother. By that
time he was drunk with traditional beer. I went
to snatch the stick and he was resisting. In the
course of that his hands slipped off the stick and
he fell back hitting his head on the floor. It was
just very unfortunate he died.

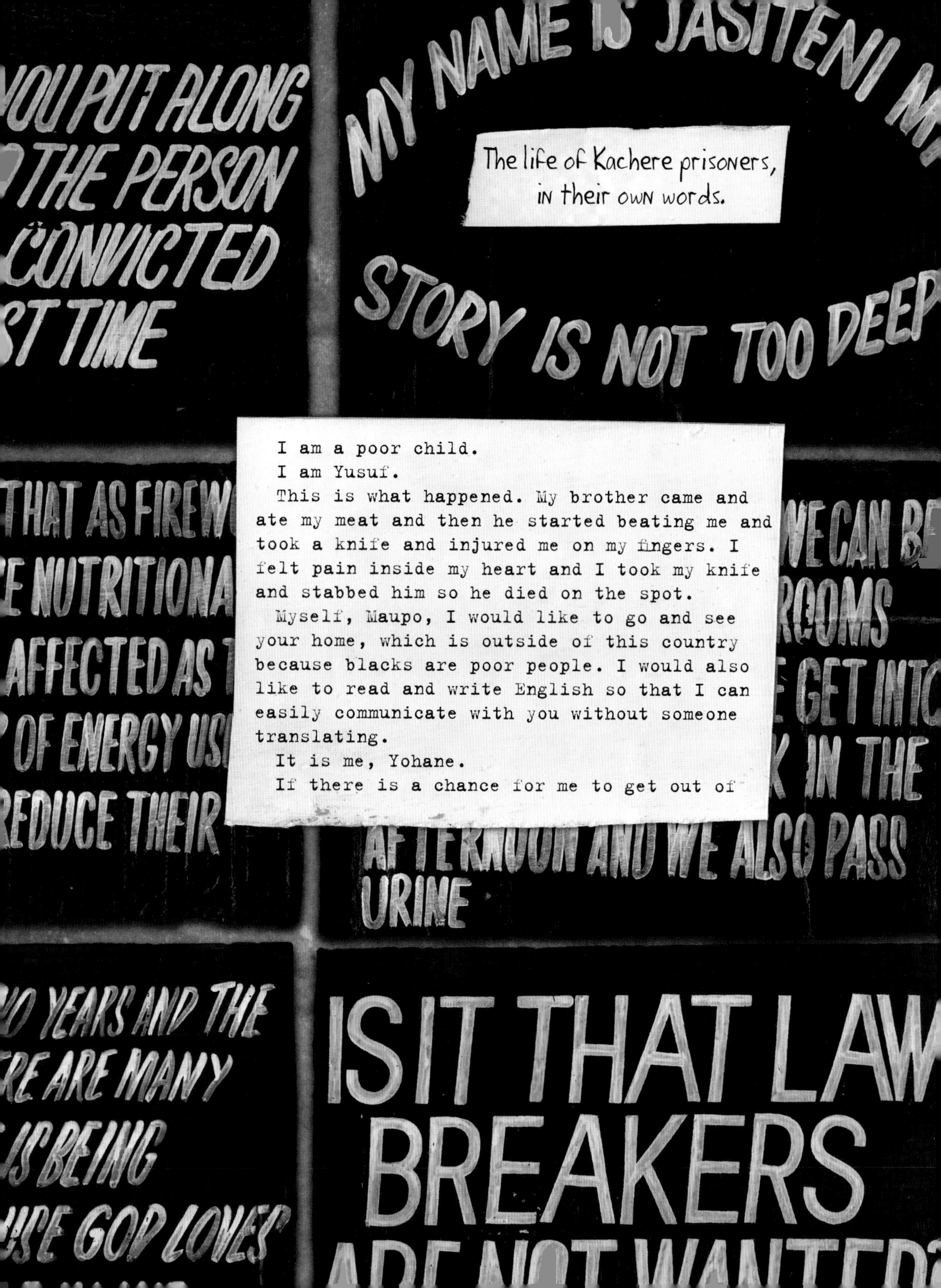

The life of Kachere prisoners, in their own words.

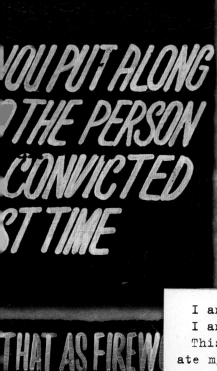

YOU PUT ALONG
THE PERSON
CONVICTED
ST TIME

STORY IS NOT TOO DEEP

THAT AS FIREW...
E NUTRITIONA...
AFFECTED AS...
OF ENERGY US...
REDUCE THEIR

VE CAN B...
ROOMS
E GET INT...
K IN THE
AFTERNOON AND WE ALSO PASS
URINE

```
I am a poor child.
I am Yusuf.
This is what happened. My brother came and
ate my meat and then he started beating me and
took a knife and injured me on my fingers. I
felt pain inside my heart and I took my knife
and stabbed him so he died on the spot.
  Myself, Maupo, I would like to go and see
your home, which is outside of this country
because blacks are poor people. I would also
like to read and write English so that I can
easily communicate with you without someone
translating.
  It is me, Yohane.
  If there is a chance for me to get out of
```

O YEARS AND THE
RE ARE MANY
IS BEING
...SE GOD LOVES

ISIT THAT LAW
BREAKERS
ARE NOT WANTED...

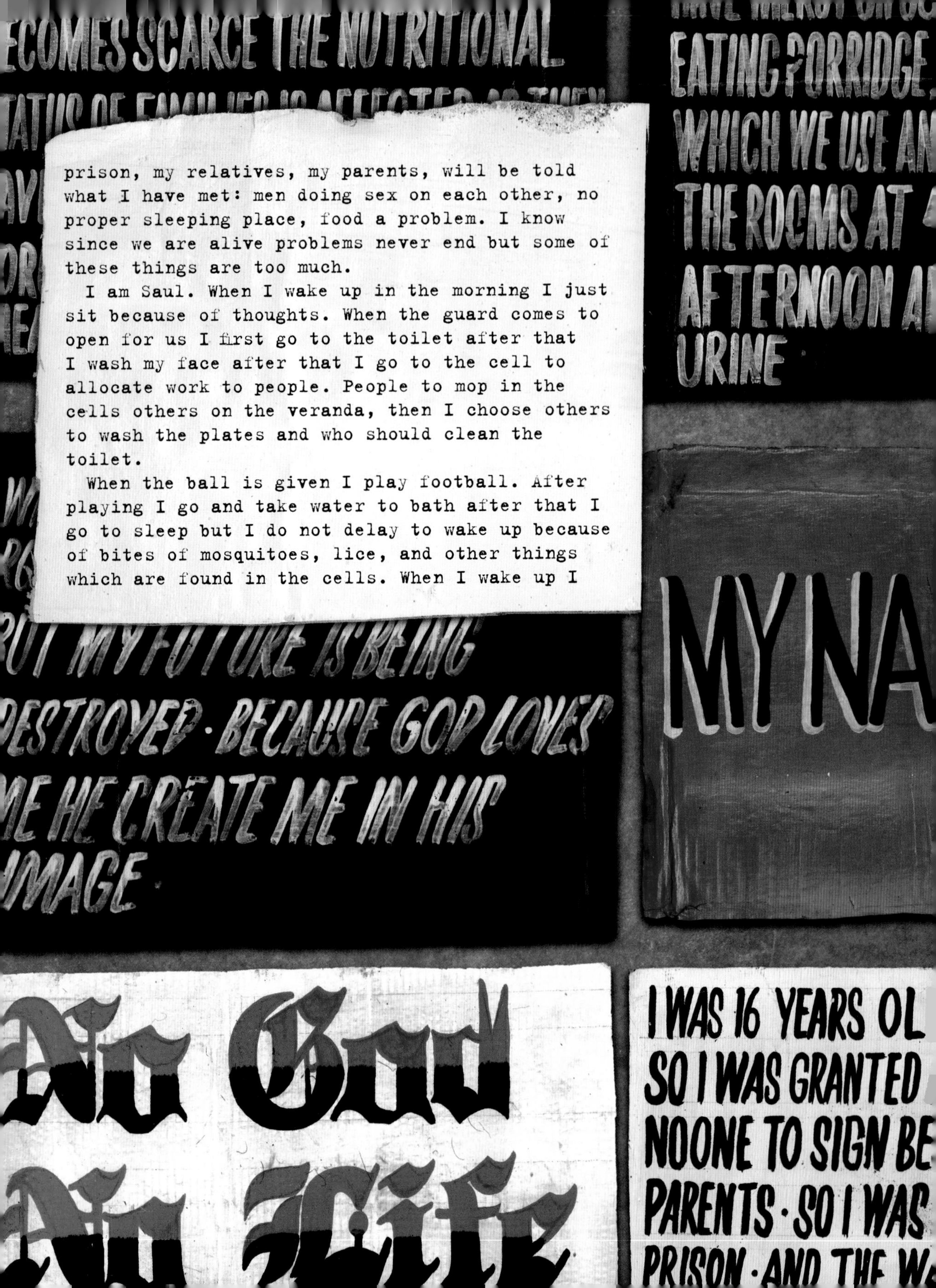
prison, my relatives, my parents, will be told what I have met: men doing sex on each other, no proper sleeping place, food a problem. I know since we are alive problems never end but some of these things are too much.

I am Saul. When I wake up in the morning I just sit because of thoughts. When the guard comes to open for us I first go to the toilet after that I wash my face after that I go to the cell to allocate work to people. People to mop in the cells others on the veranda, then I choose others to wash the plates and who should clean the toilet.

When the ball is given I play football. After playing I go and take water to bath after that I go to sleep but I do not delay to wake up because of bites of mosquitoes, lice, and other things which are found in the cells. When I wake up I

ECOMES SCARCE THE NUTRITIONAL
EATING PORRIDGE,
WHICH WE USE AN
THE ROOMS AT 4
AFTERNOON A
URINE
UT MY FUTURE IS BEING
DESTROYED · BECAUSE GOD LOVES
ME HE CREATE ME IN HIS
IMAGE
MY NA
No God
No Life
I WAS 16 YEARS OL
SO I WAS GRANTED
NOONE TO SIGN BE
PARENTS · SO I WAS
PRISON · AND THE W

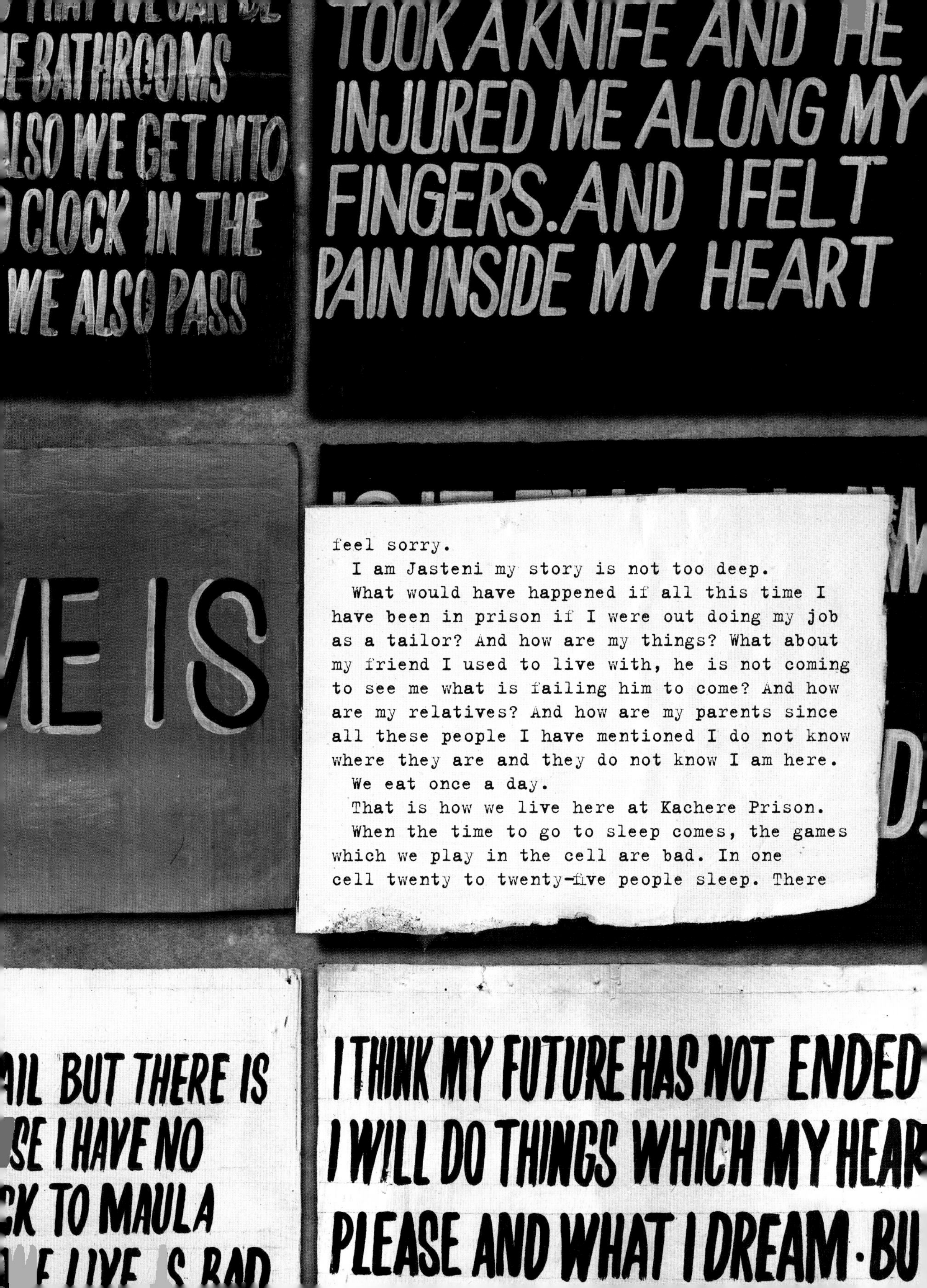
E BATHROOMS
LSO WE GET INTO
CLOCK IN THE
WE ALSO PASS
TOOK A KNIFE AND HE
INJURED ME ALONG MY
FINGERS. AND I FELT
PAIN INSIDE MY HEART
ME IS
IL BUT THERE IS
SE I HAVE NO
CK TO MAULA
I THINK MY FUTURE HAS NOT ENDED
I WILL DO THINGS WHICH MY HEAR
PLEASE AND WHAT I DREAM · BU

feel sorry.

I am Jasteni my story is not too deep.

What would have happened if all this time I have been in prison if I were out doing my job as a tailor? And how are my things? What about my friend I used to live with, he is not coming to see me what is failing him to come? And how are my relatives? And how are my parents since all these people I have mentioned I do not know where they are and they do not know I am here.

We eat once a day.

That is how we live here at Kachere Prison.

When the time to go to sleep comes, the games which we play in the cell are bad. In one cell twenty to twenty-five people sleep. There

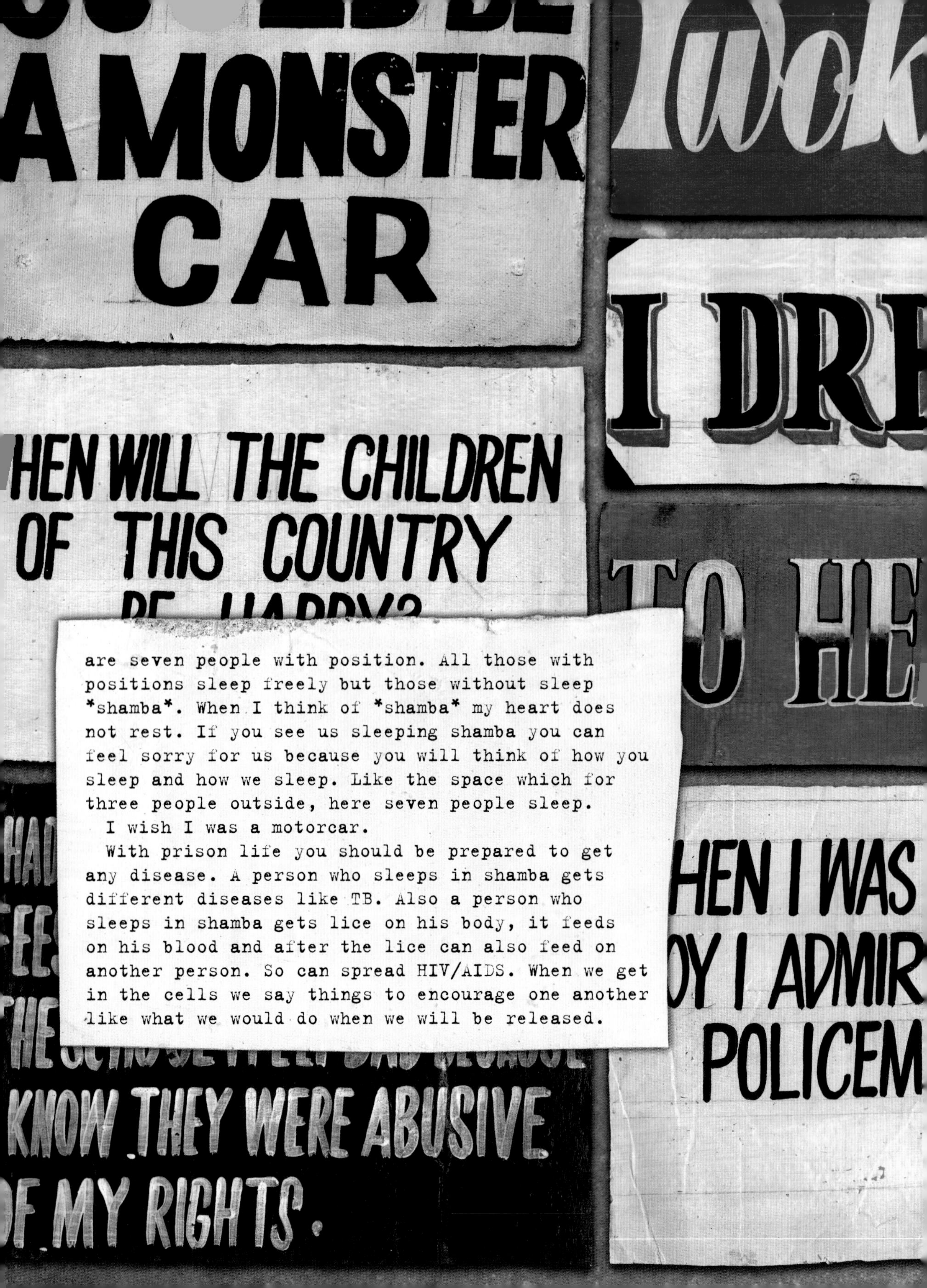
A MONSTER
CAR
HEN WILL THE CHILDREN
OF THIS COUNTRY
I DR
TO HE
HEN I WAS
OY I ADMIR
POLICEM
KNOW THEY WERE ABUSIVE
F MY RIGHTS.

are seven people with position. All those with positions sleep freely but those without sleep *shamba*. When I think of *shamba* my heart does not rest. If you see us sleeping shamba you can feel sorry for us because you will think of how you sleep and how we sleep. Like the space which for three people outside, here seven people sleep.

I wish I was a motorcar.

With prison life you should be prepared to get any disease. A person who sleeps in shamba gets different diseases like TB. Also a person who sleeps in shamba gets lice on his body, it feeds on his blood and after the lice can also feed on another person. So can spread HIV/AIDS. When we get in the cells we say things to encourage one another like what we would do when we will be released.

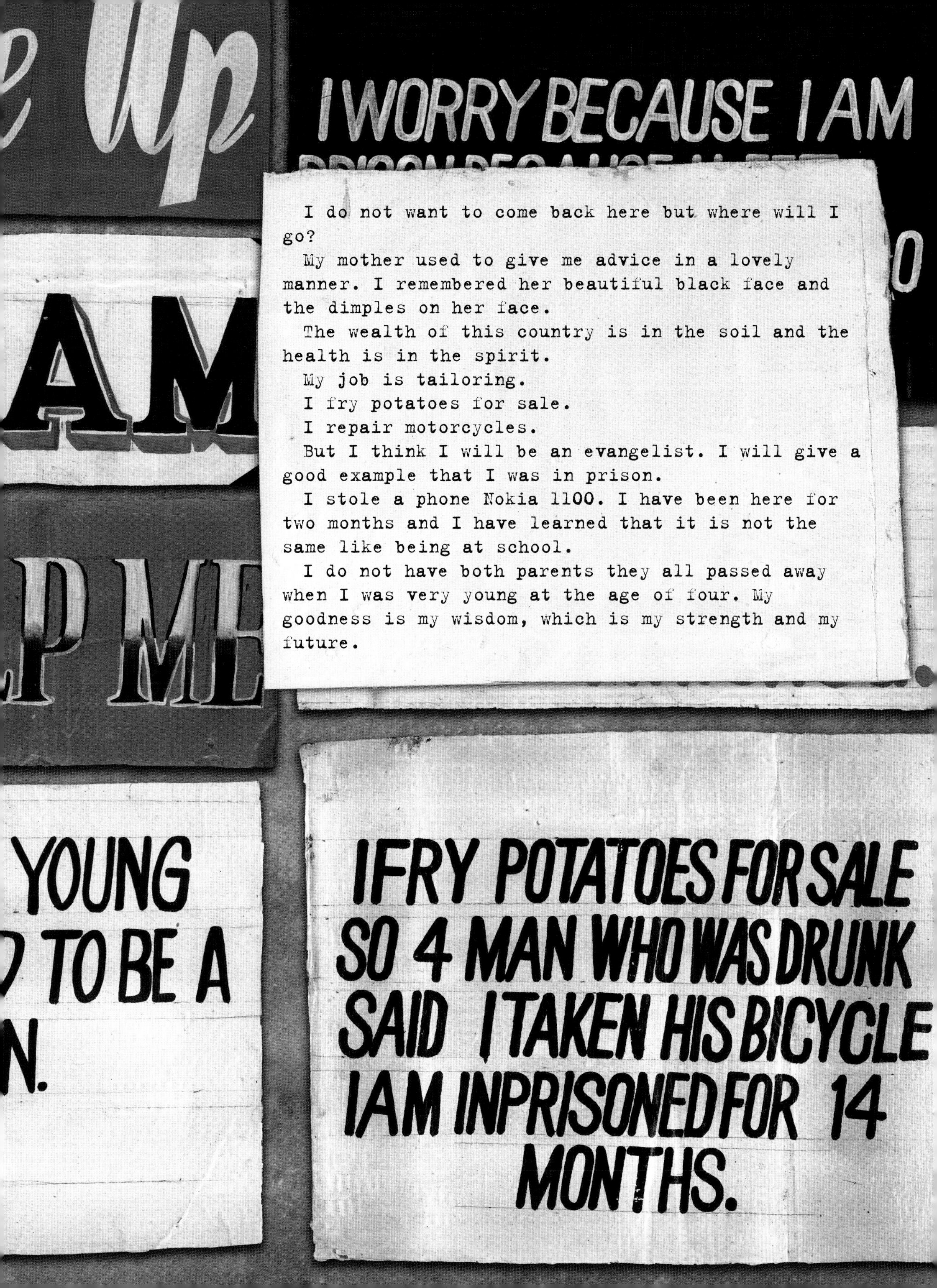
I do not want to come back here but where will I go?

My mother used to give me advice in a lovely manner. I remembered her beautiful black face and the dimples on her face.

The wealth of this country is in the soil and the health is in the spirit.

My job is tailoring.

I fry potatoes for sale.

I repair motorcycles.

But I think I will be an evangelist. I will give a good example that I was in prison.

I stole a phone Nokia 1100. I have been here for two months and I have learned that it is not the same like being at school.

I do not have both parents they all passed away when I was very young at the age of four. My goodness is my wisdom, which is my strength and my future.

Up
I WORRY BECAUSE I AM
AM
YOUNG
TO BE A
N.
I FRY POTATOES FOR SALE
SO 4 MAN WHO WAS DRUNK
SAID I TAKEN HIS BICYCLE
IAM INPRISONED FOR 14
MONTHS.

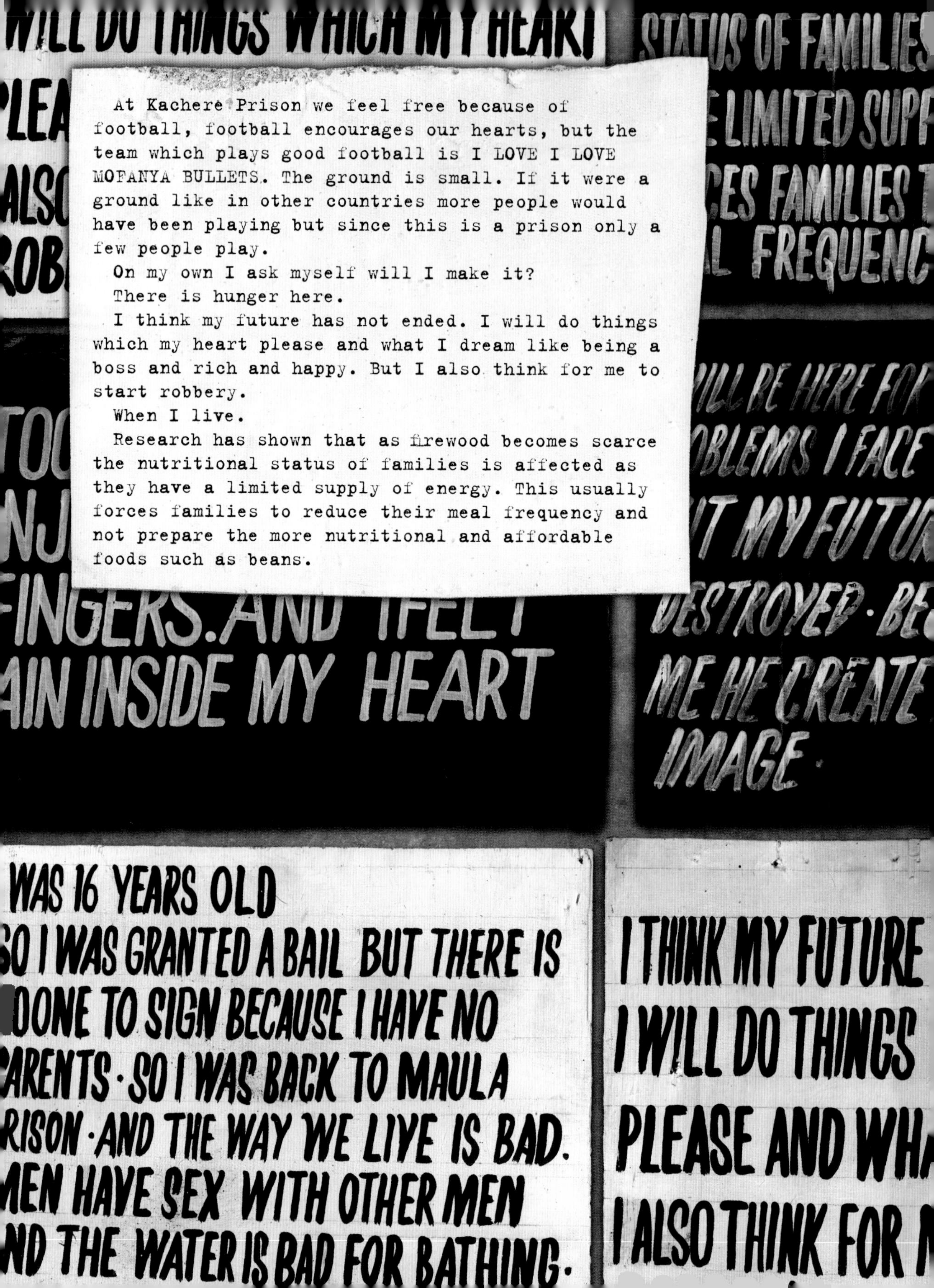

At Kachere Prison we feel free because of football, football encourages our hearts, but the team which plays good football is I LOVE I LOVE MOFANYA BULLETS. The ground is small. If it were a ground like in other countries more people would have been playing but since this is a prison only a few people play.

On my own I ask myself will I make it?

There is hunger here.

I think my future has not ended. I will do things which my heart please and what I dream like being a boss and rich and happy. But I also think for me to start robbery.

When I live.

Research has shown that as firewood becomes scarce the nutritional status of families is affected as they have a limited supply of energy. This usually forces families to reduce their meal frequency and not prepare the more nutritional and affordable foods such as beans.

WILL DO THINGS WHICH MY HEART
STATUS OF FAMILIES
LIMITED SUPP
CES FAMILIES T
L FREQUENC
ILL BE HERE FOR
OBLEMS I FACE
T MY FUTUR
DESTROYED · BE
ME HE CREATE
IMAGE ·
INGERS. AND I FELT
AIN INSIDE MY HEART
WAS 16 YEARS OLD
SO I WAS GRANTED A BAIL BUT THERE IS
ONE TO SIGN BECAUSE I HAVE NO
ARENTS · SO I WAS BACK TO MAULA
RISON · AND THE WAY WE LIVE IS BAD.
MEN HAVE SEX WITH OTHER MEN
ND THE WATER IS BAD FOR BATHING.
I THINK MY FUTURE
I WILL DO THINGS
PLEASE AND WHA
I ALSO THINK FOR

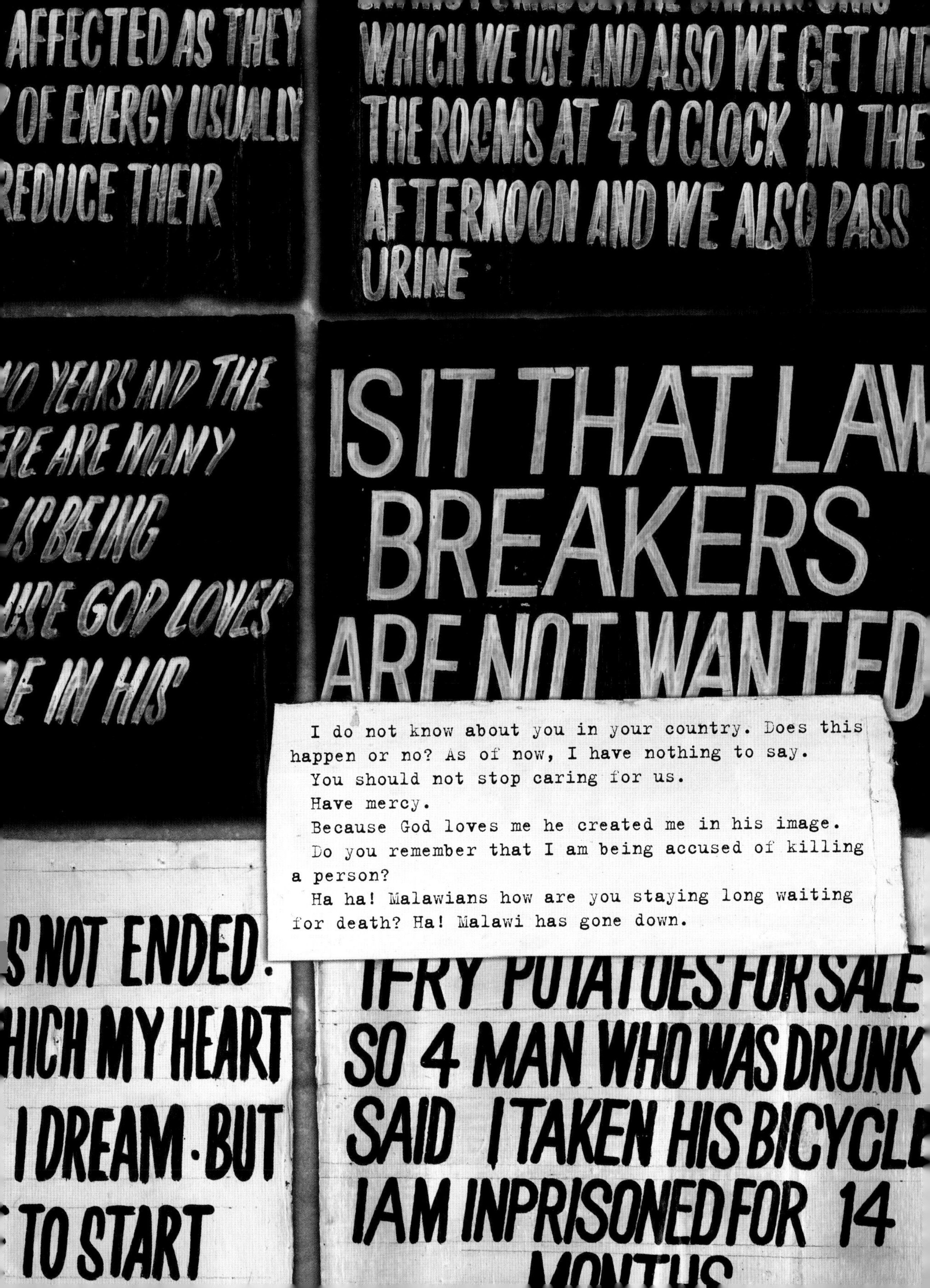
AFFECTED AS THEY
OF ENERGY USUALLY
REDUCE THEIR
WHICH WE USE AND ALSO WE GET INT
THE ROOMS AT 4 O CLOCK IN THE
AFTERNOON AND WE ALSO PASS
URINE
YEARS AND THE
ERE ARE MANY
IS BEING
USE GOD LOVES
E IN HIS
IS IT THAT LAW
BREAKERS
ARE NOT WANTED
I do not know about you in your country. Does this happen or no? As of now, I have nothing to say.
You should not stop caring for us.
Have mercy.
Because God loves me he created me in his image.
Do you remember that I am being accused of killing a person?
Ha ha! Malawians how are you staying long waiting for death? Ha! Malawi has gone down.
S NOT ENDED.
HICH MY HEART
I DREAM. BUT
TO START
FRY POTATOES FOR SALE
SO 4 MAN WHO WAS DRUNK
SAID I TAKEN HIS BICYCLE
I AM INPRISONED FOR 14

When I was little, I always imagined that I'd find him. I-Z-H-O-U. My grandmother's son. Maybe he only got lost in the crowd, but they never killed him, he survived the gas chambers and grew up and he's safe and everything is okay.

It's time to stop hoping for that. There are no records of Izhou's birth or death. And I no longer have any trouble understanding that a person can disappear completely.

Ingushetia, Burma, Juárez, Malawi. I'm left with this kaleidoscope of sensations and images. Child soldiers trying not to cry, my own heart lurching. Fear at the edge of an empty space in Mexico. Miriam and Sunshine. The sound of rats on a metal roof, startling that specific silence that accompanies loneliness.

Now what?

I spend my last day in Malawi in a tiny cell at the back of the prison.

I notice the rock. I first noticed its presence on my second day at Kachere. Larger than my palm, it was heavy, with sharp jutting angles. I had been talking with a boy convicted of killing his brother. The boy had a head shaped like a zucchini and eyes on a diagonal slope. As he spoke, his restless hands picked at scabs between his toes. The smell of shit was as sharp as the claustrophobic stench of illness in the airless room. My eyes traveled to the rock. The guards had vanished and we were completely alone.

I wondered what would happen with this rock. Would it be taken away? Would one of the boys use it against the guards or in self-defense during a fight?

A rock is a weapon.

Yet here it is, in the same place as it was days before.

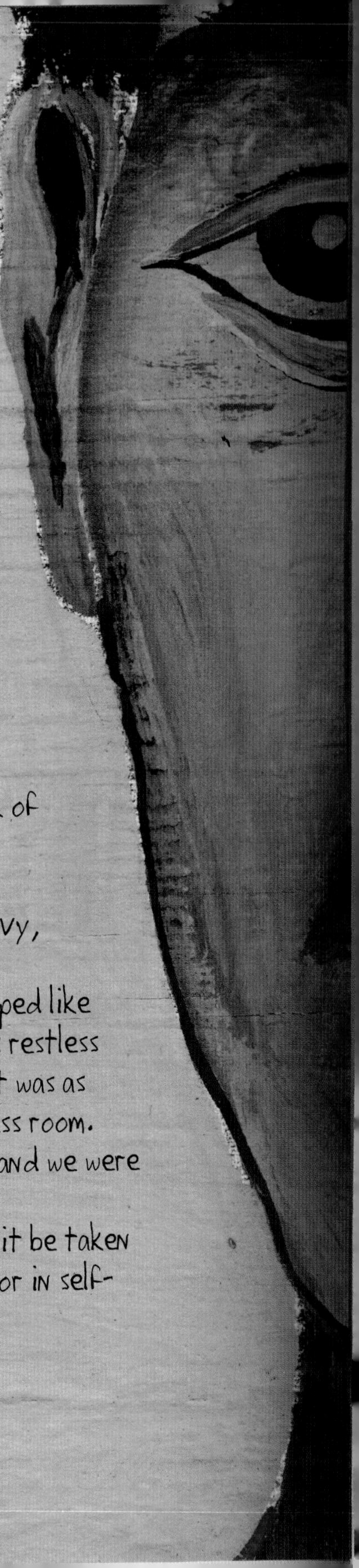

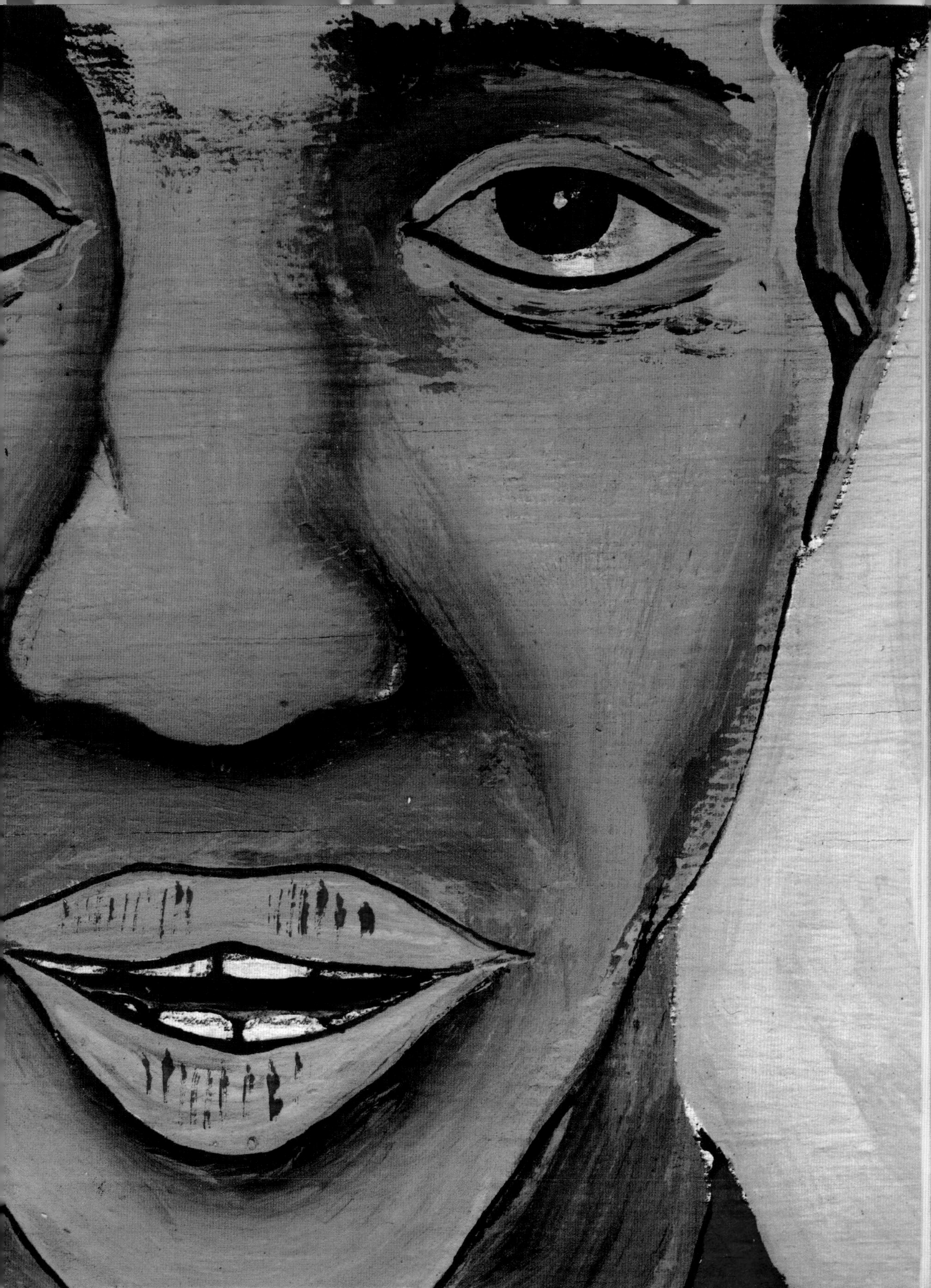

About 10 boys have volunteered to paint. I spread a set of wooden boards out on the floor of the cell. A sign painter has come along with me to teach the boys painting technique. As soon as the painter arrived, though, he began to sketch the prison walls.

The smell of wood and paint begins to fill the cell.

One of the boys, mentally challenged and accused of murder, has oversize hands that can't quite grip the pencil. His drawing is just a series of scribbles punctuated with harsh black dots at each place where he broke the pencil lead. He's frustrated. He is sliding his feet along the gravel and blinking quickly. His breath moving faster.

I show him my own attempt to draw the cell with its stained walls and patchy concrete. It's really terrible. Do his eyes seem to light up?

Then he begins to outline his foot, slowly, painstakingly. I begin to copy him, tracing my own hand. We drift away into the sound of wet paint hitting wood and the deep sighs of boys totally lost.

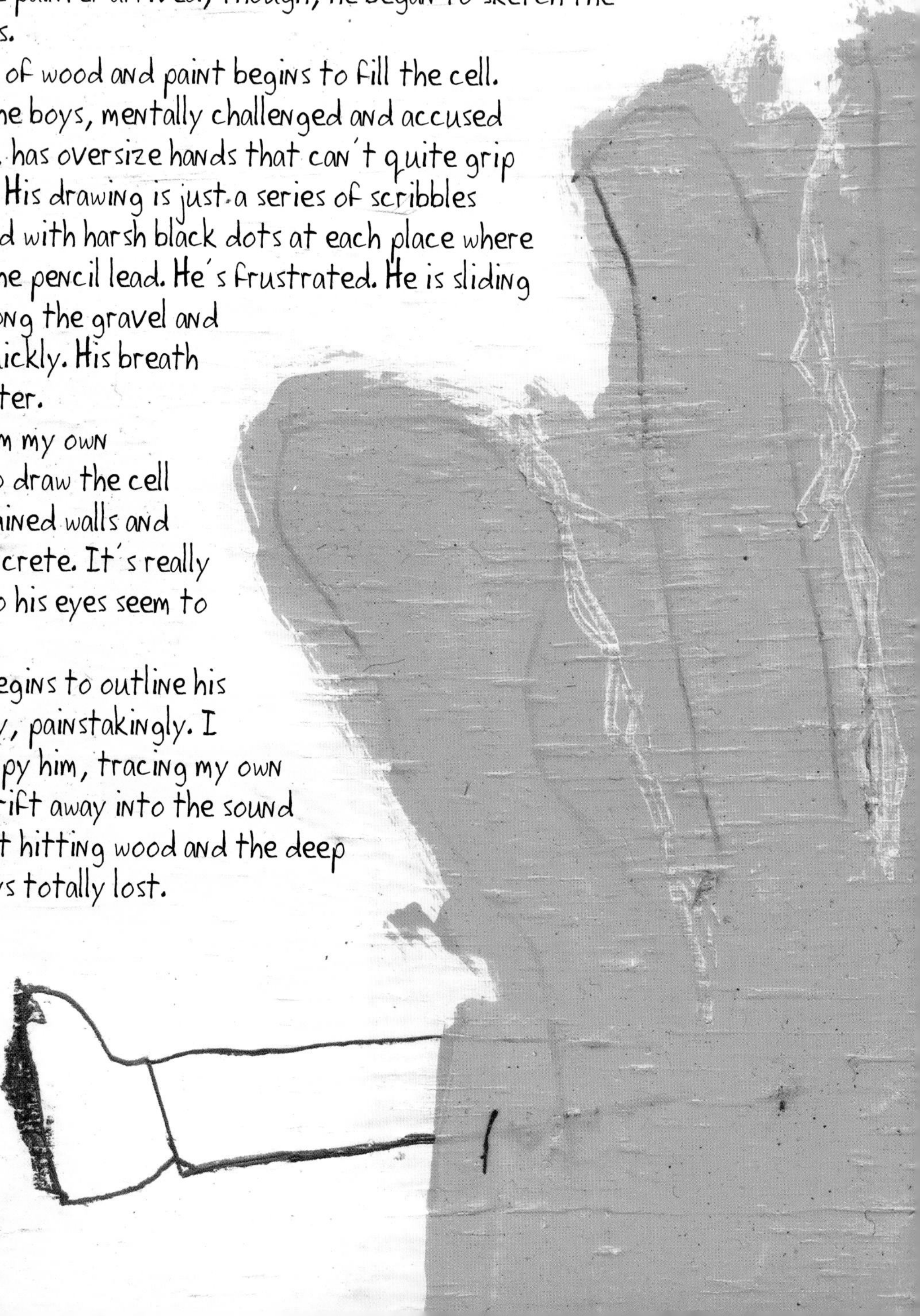

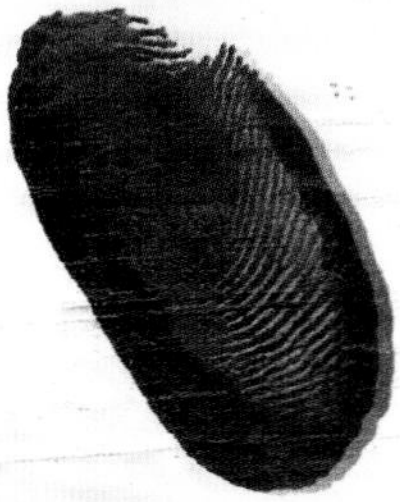

Then the boy holds up his painting. He has painted both his feet on the board - one is blue, and for the other he's mixed yellow and brown to make saffron. It's yellow, he says, because his foot is like the sun. He is shaking his head from side to side and his mouth keeps on spontaneously opening, a tiny smile escaping.

It's beautiful.

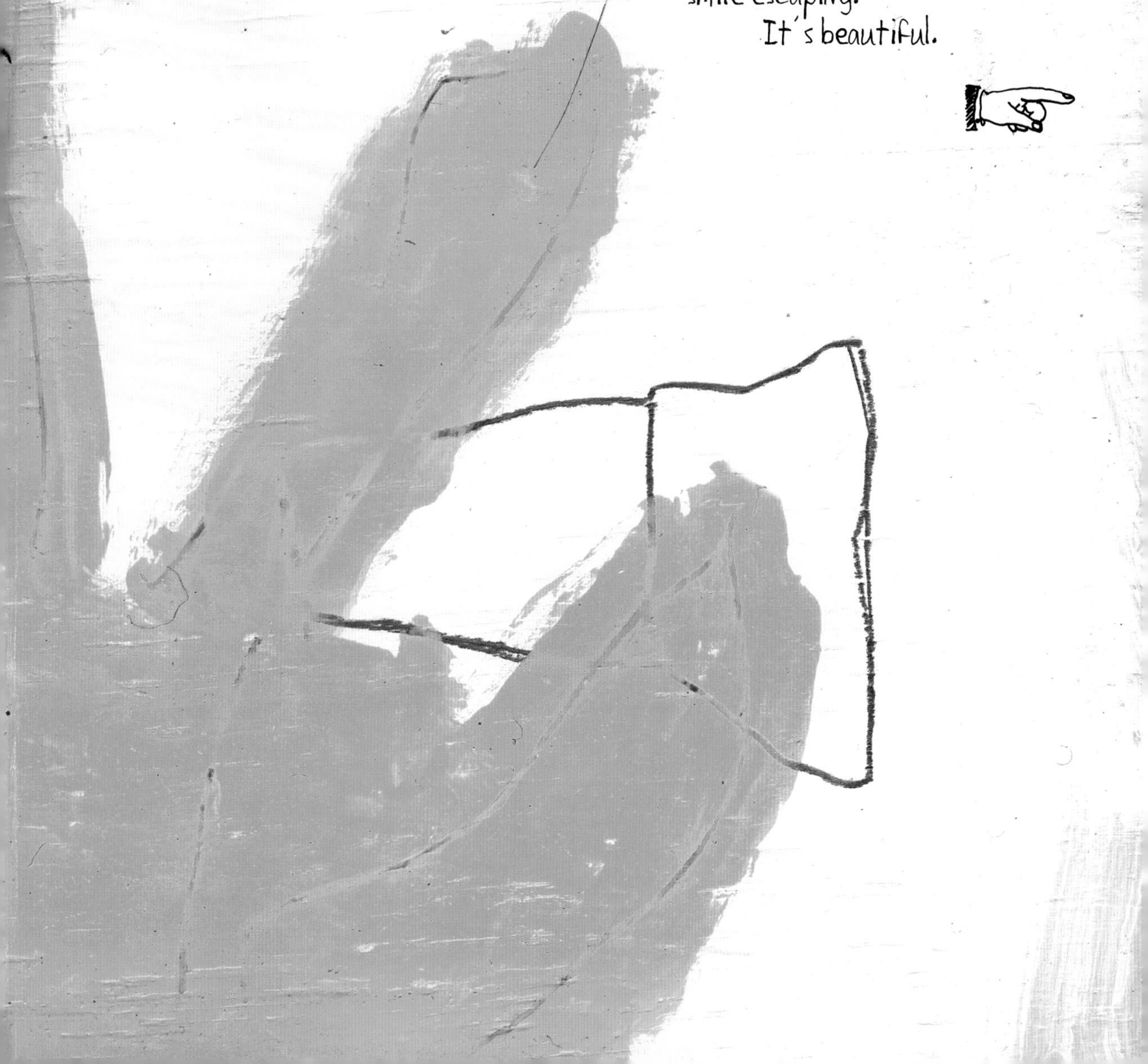

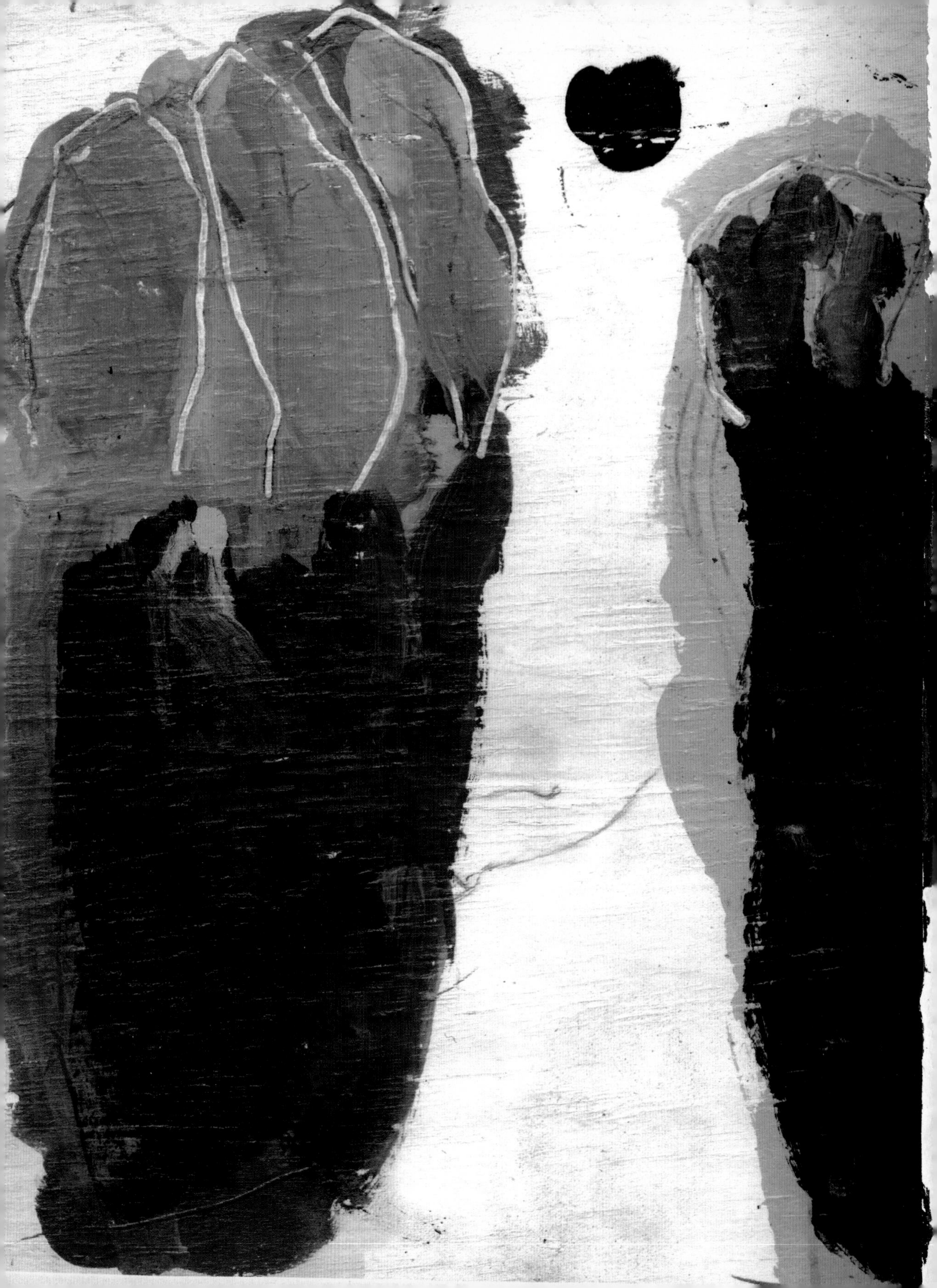